Getting Started in Business Plans

2nd Edition

by Veechi Curtis, MBA

T0370154

for dummies®

A Wiley Brand

Getting Started in Business Plans For Dummies®, 2nd Edition

Published by
John Wiley & Sons, Australia Ltd
Level 4, 600 Bourke Street
Melbourne, Vic 3000
www.dummies.com
Copyright © 2025 John Wiley & Sons, Australia Ltd
The moral rights of the author have been asserted.
ISBN: 978-1-394-23734-0

A catalogue record for this book is available from the National Library of Australia

Registered Office
John Wiley & Sons Australia, Ltd. Level 4, 600 Bourke Street, Melbourne, VIC 3000, Australia

For details of our global editorial offices, customer services, and more information about Wiley products visit us at www.wiley.com.

Wiley also publishes its books in a variety of electronic formats and by print-on-demand. Some content that appears in standard print versions of this book may not be available in other formats.

Cover Image: © Zamrznuti tonovi/Adobe Stock Photos

Typeset by Straive

SKYB152A624-A14A-4716-811F-CD39439455D0_041125

Contents at a Glance

Table of Contents

Introduction

I grew up in Scotland, where the winters can be wild, wet, and cold. My father was a self-employed landscape gardener and, each year, as the days grew shorter, he would start hatching entrepreneurial plots to see the family through the scant earnings of the winter months. Handmade garden furniture, barrels from the local brewery scrubbed back and filled with violets, gold-leaf mirror restoration and beach-scavenged scallop shells were but a few of the ill-fated ventures that would transform our Victorian flat into a hive of industry for a few fleeting months of each year.

I started my first business at the age of 26 and have been in business ever since, oscillating in a manner not unlike my father's between the more stable income of business consulting and the somewhat precarious existence of writing and publishing.

Yet when working on this book, I realized something quite fundamental. While I've been steadily successful for more than 20 years, all too often the sensible-cardigan-wearing-accountant side of me wins out against the risk-taking-creative-why-don't-we-try-this side of me. Possibly due to the rather feast-and-famine finances of my childhood, I typically spend more time analyzing profit margins than I do thinking of creative new products; I focus more on managing risk than being a trendsetter. If you've been in business before, I'm sure you too have experienced this natural tension between your entrepreneurial side and the inner voice of 'reason'.

One challenge for me in writing this book has been to find ways to encourage dreams to flourish while simultaneously exploring the somewhat sobering process of writing a business plan. I'm writing this introduction having just finished the last chapter of this book and, happily, I think that the process has worked on me. I'm itching with impatience to begin my next business venture, and feel utterly optimistic about its prospects. (I remain my father's daughter, after all.)

I hope you have a similar experience with this book, and that I share enough inspiration for your inner entrepreneur to thrive while at the same time providing unshakeable feet-on-the-ground practicality.

About This Book

I like to think that this book is a bit different from other business planning books, not least because this book is part of the *For Dummies* series. *Dummies* books aren't about thinking that you're a 'dummy' — far from it. What the *For Dummies* series is all about is balancing heavyweight topics with a lightweight mindset, and sharing a 'can-do' attitude that encourages anyone — no matter how young or old, how inexperienced or how veteran — to give the subject at hand a go.

I like to think that the *Dummies* way of thinking has helped me to bring a fresh approach to the subject of business planning. I've tried not to get bogged down in the same old stodgy discussions of mission statements, values and organizational charts; instead, I've focused more on working with others, being creative and thinking of your business as something that's unique and separate from yourself.

You may be surprised by the fact that I devote five whole chapters to the topic of finance (you'll only find one finance chapter in most business planning books). I'm a real advocate of the importance of financial planning and, in this book, I try to break the topic down into bite-sized chunks that anyone can understand, even if they haven't done any bookkeeping or accounting before.

I also understand that most people who've worked in business end up with knowledge that's patchy. You may know heaps about marketing but nothing about finance, or vice versa. The beauty of *Dummies* books is that you can just leap in, find the chunk of information that addresses your query, and start reading from there.

One more thing. Throughout this book you'll see sidebars — text that sits in a separate box with gray shading. Think of sidebars as the nut topping on your ice-cream: Nice to have, but not essential. Feel free to skip these bits.

Foolish Assumptions

When writing this book, I make no assumptions about your prior experience. Maybe you've been in business all your life or maybe you've never been in business before. It could be that you're a tech geek or it's possible that you hate computers. Maybe you love numbers or — much more likely — you may have a somewhat queasy feeling when it comes to math.

I also make no assumptions about the age of your business, and realize that for many people reading this book, your business is still a seedling waiting to be watered. (For this reason, I include practical advice such as how to budget for personal expenses while you're building your business, and why things such as your relationships and family situation are all part of the picture.)

Last, I don't try to guess where you live in the world. After all, the principles of business planning are universal, whether you're in the snowdrifts of Alaska, the stone country of Australia, or the kilt-swaying highlands of Scotland.

Icons Used in This Book

REMEMBER

Tie a knot in that elephant's trunk, pin an egg timer to your shirt but, whatever you do, don't forget the pointers next to this icon.

TIP

This icon points to ways to give your business plan that extra spark.

TRUE
STORY

Real-life stories from others who've been there and done that.

WARNING

A pitfall for the unwary. Read these warnings carefully.

Where to Go from Here

Getting Started in Business Plans For Dummies, 2nd edition, is no page-turning thriller (probably a good thing given the subject matter) and doesn't require you to start at the beginning and follow through to the end. Instead, feel free to jump in and start reading from whatever section is most relevant to you:

New to business and you've never created a business plan before? I suggest you read Chapters 1, 2 and 3 before doing much else. Chapter 1 provides an overview for creating your plan, and Chapters 2 and 3 help you to consolidate your business concept. From here, you're probably best to read the chapters in the order that I present them, because these chapters follow the same sequence as the topics within a business plan.

If business strategy is more your concern, Chapters 2 to 5 and 11 are the places to be.

Are financial projections a source of woe? Chapters 7 to 11 are here to help.

For advice on creating a plan that can't fail to impress prospective lenders or investors, Chapter 12 explains how to pull your plan together. And, finally, Chapter 13 provides advice and encouragement if things aren't looking as good as you'd hoped.

IN THIS CHAPTER

» **Getting started without another moment's hesitation**

» **Deciding what elements to include in your plan**

» **Understanding why business planning is harder than it looks**

» **Tricking yourself into doing the deed**

Chapter **1**
Letting Your Plan Take Flight

A business plan is as much a way of thinking as it is a document. Some of the most important elements of a business plan can be done while talking with colleagues, walking along the beach, or taking time out over a cup of coffee.

Key to a business planning mindset is a willingness to be objective about strategy, the ability to think of your business as something that's separate from you, and the discipline to analyze your financials (even if you're not naturally good with numbers).

Importantly, a business plan doesn't necessarily require days or weeks of your time. I often recommend to people they approach their plan in bite-sized chunks, whether this be redesigning pricing strategies, spending time researching competitors, or experimenting with different pricing models.

In this chapter, I talk about who a business plan is for, what goes into a plan, and how you might start thinking about your business model. I also explain why it can be hard to be objective and motivated about planning for your business, and share a few insights into how to keep yourself on track.

Getting Your Feet Wet

In *Getting Started in Business Plans For Dummies*, 2nd edition, I place less emphasis on the importance of creating a written plan and more on why planning is best viewed as a frame of mind. The neat thing about this way of thinking is that you can start with your plan at any time, even if you know you have only one hour free this week and you're flying overseas for a holiday the next.

Planning can even be fun once you get started. Some of my best business ideas have come to me while lying in the hammock on holidays, digging up weeds in the garden, or having a quiet coffee.

Choosing your dance partners

Unless you've run a business before, creating a business plan almost certainly needs a little help from outside. The good news is that all you have to do is ask. Consider the following sources:

TIP

>> **Business planning courses:** In my opinion, a structured course spread over several weeks or even months is the very best possible way to accumulate basic planning skills. Not only do you have the discipline of working on your plan at least once a week, but you also usually receive expert mentoring from the teacher or teachers, as well as peer support from other people in a similar position to you.

>> **Business advisory centers:** Depending on where you are in the world, business advisory centers have different names and structures. However, most state and federal governments fund some form of free advisory center.

>> **Business consultants:** While I warn against delegating the whole planning process to outsiders, expert consultants can be a great resource, especially if you retain control and ownership of your plan.

>> **Your accountant:** I strongly recommend that you do your own financial projections, rather than delegating this task to a bookkeeper or accountant. (I explain just how in Chapters 7 through to 11.) However, after you have made your best attempt, consider asking your accountant to review your figures, and help you to identify anything that doesn't make sense or seems unrealistic.

>> **Your lawyer:** Your lawyer is an excellent source of advice for managing risk, in particular for protecting your name and your brand, limiting liability through company structures, or reviewing contracts.

>> **Friends and family:** Not only is the advice of friends and family usually free, but these people also understand you like nobody else. Support and encouragement from friends and family is invaluable on those doubtful days when you think you (and your new business idea) may be crazy.

>> **Your spouse/life partner:** Last but not least. Need I say more?

REMEMBER

Even if you don't have all of the skills required to create a plan, you won't find a better motivator for acquiring these skills than the feast-and-famine of your business venture. Experience is a generous teacher.

Deciding who this plan is for

The easy answer to the question of who your plan is for is you, of course. Your plan is an ongoing process, not a massive document that you create every year or so. When you create a business plan for your own use only, you can pick a structure, time and format that work well for you.

Of course, in real life the impetus for most business plans is to seek capital, either from an investor or via a bank loan. In Chapter 12, I explain how to frame your plan according to your audience: Investors are typically more interested in a high rate of return and the excitement of a clever business idea; banks are usually more interested in collateral, consistent trading results and your personal credit rating.

WARNING

Regardless of who is likely to read your plan, I strongly suggest that when it comes to the financials — sales targets, income projections, profit projections and so on — you be consistent. Don't have one version of financials for your own purposes, and another spruced-up version for the bank. Instead, stay as realistic as possible. This tactic helps you gain respect from any likely investors and keeps you grounded as to what lies ahead.

Subscribing to a planning app

In this book, I try to provide you with all the information you need to build your plan. You may be wondering how to use this book alongside the many business planning apps available.

Even with this book to hand, a business planning app undoubtedly makes the process easier. Apps such as Bizplan, Enloop, LivePlan and PlanGuru help you to structure each section of your plan, can offer suggested wording based on your industry, and are excellent for creating financial forecasts, particularly if numbers don't come naturally to you.

TIP

I suggest you weigh up the pros and cons for yourself by subscribing to a service such as www.liveplan.com for a month or so. The monthly fee is usually fairly modest, and represents a small financial commitment for what is potentially a significant saving of your time.

I've written this book so it can go hand in hand with any business planning app, aiming to provide guidance as to what's important, and what's not. For example, almost anyone can explain the concept of strategic advantage in a few sentences, and most planning apps simply provide a definition, followed by a template where you can write your own. However, in real life, I find that strategic advantage is super tricky to understand and it's for this reason that I devote two whole chapters to the subject (Chapters 2 and 3), highlighting how fundamental this concept is to business success.

ARE YOU READY?

I find that if someone really wants to start their own business, wild horses can't hold them back. The idea keeps coming around and around until that person finally takes the leap and says, 'I'm going to give it a go'.

So if you're champing at the bit to start your new business, I have just three questions to ask you first:

- Do you have experience in the kind of business you're planning to start? For example, if you're looking at buying a coffee van, have you actually spent a few weeks selling coffee in this way? Do you have barista or retail experience?

- Do you definitely have enough capital to get started? If you're not sure, do you think you may be better saving for a while before you launch your business? (See Chapter 7 for more on budgeting for start-up expenses.)
- Is your partner/spouse/family supportive of this venture?

If your answer to any of these questions is 'no', I suggest that you try to temper your enthusiasm just a little. And if you still can't wait, hey, I completely understand.

Structuring Your Plan

The best business plan format for a company with a turnover of $100 million and 200 employees is going to be utterly different from the best format for a start-up business with no employees. For this reason, you can find as many possible formats for a business plan as recipes for Bolognese sauce.

Most formats, however, have certain key elements in common, although the sequence of these elements varies. These key elements are as follows:

>> **A cover page and table of contents.**

>> **An Executive Summary.** I explain how to write this in Chapter 12.

>> **Your point of difference and strategic advantage (usually but not always part of your Executive Summary).** For more on these topics, see Chapters 2 and 3.

>> **Your vision for the future.** Although I devote most of a chapter to this topic (see Chapter 3), the aim is to distil this vision into a sentence or two, either as part of your Executive Summary, or part of your pitch for funding.

>> **A SWOT analysis.** I cover this topic in Chapter 5.

>> **A competitor analysis and marketing plan.** Chapter 3 talks about competitor analysis and competitive strategy, and Chapter 6 provides a complete summary of how to construct a marketing plan.

» **A people plan.** A business isn't anything without the people who run it, and your skills, entrepreneurialism, and natural abilities are as much a part of the mix as anything else, as are the skills of the people you choose to involve in your business. This part of your plan needs to outline the people element of your business: Who does what, and why they're the best choice for the job.

Even if you don't have any employees yet, you can still include details about any consultants, advisers, mentors, or professionals who you plan to involve in your business. These details help to establish credibility for anybody else reading your plan, and prompt you to think further outside the business than just yourself.

Chapter 2 touches on this topic, while Chapter 4 explores the people side of your plan in more depth. (People planning doesn't necessarily take a huge amount of time at first, but is something that can be a huge time-waster if you don't get it right.)

» **A risk-management plan, if appropriate.** The more risk in your business, the more important it is to include a risk-management strategy in your plan.

» **A summary of operations, if appropriate.** I talk about how to write this summary in Chapter 12.

» **Financial reports.** For most new businesses, the financial part of your plan may be as simple as a Profit & Loss Projection for the next 12 months. Established businesses may include projections for 24 or 36 months ahead, as well as historical Profit & Loss reports and Balance Sheets for the previous year or years. Financials often also include break-even analysis, Cashflow Projections, and budgets.

For more on creating a Profit & Loss Projection, see Chapters 8 through to 11.

TIP

For new or growing businesses that require a certain sales volume before the model becomes profitable, I suggest you extend your projections for at least a couple of years to demonstrate the long-term viability of your concept.

» **The ask.** I talk more about asking for money in Chapter 12.

If you feel daunted by the preceding list, I suggest you start with the basics: Your point of difference, a SWOT analysis, a marketing plan, and a Profit & Loss Projection for the next 12 months. With these elements in place, you can return to complete more details in your plan as soon as you have the stamina.

Getting Beyond First Base

We humans often like to stick with what we know and what feels right — and business plans are no exception. In this section, I delve into the psychology of business plans, focusing on how human bias and subconscious behaviors can serve to undermine the objectivity so essential to good planning.

Guarding against optimism

People often ascribe the high failure rates of venture capital to perceived levels of risk, and proof that the system is working as it should. However, I'd argue that these failure rates have more to do with the nature of what it means to be human. Specifically, we humans are an overly optimistic bunch, with subconscious instincts that often override rational decision-making.

The majority of humans are endowed with something known as *optimism bias* — the tendency to overestimate the likelihood of positive events, and underestimate the likelihood of negative events. And, as someone who has spent their life around entrepreneurs, I reckon the average business owner has optimism bias on steroids.

Of course, optimism is one thing, but wearing blinkers is another. How can you temper such optimism, along with other unconscious biases, to ensure your business plan is as good as can be? In this section, I consider how some innate and completely normal human behaviors might affect your ability to create a smart business plan.

Confirmation bias

Humans love *confirmation bias* — that inexorable pull that makes us look for evidence to validate what we already think, and disregard information supporting other points of view. (Next time you're making a decision or expressing an opinion about something, see if you can spot your own confirmation bias. Perhaps you like to you seek out stories that confirm your political viewpoint? Or you cling to one-off customer anecdotes that validate your new idea, and dismiss negative customer reviews that suggest otherwise?)

Confirmation bias is, of course, counter-productive to creating a business plan, particularly if you're seeking fresh ideas or wanting to assess the potential of a new business model.

REMEMBER

When creating your business plan, be wary of placing too much emphasis on information that reinforces your existing beliefs. Try to involve outside advisers during the information-gathering stage, perhaps even seeking out those who you know are likely to challenge or disagree with you. (Chapter 5 provides some good frameworks for this information-gathering process.)

The planning fallacy

The *planning fallacy* is a concept developed by Daniel Kahneman and Amos Tversky in 1979, and outlines the predisposition of humans to be overly optimistic about timelines or planning outcomes, even in the face of more general knowledge or past experience that would suggest otherwise.

The planning fallacy is most likely to arise when we trust our intuition and disregard past experience. Unfortunately, because planning is inherently about the future, we're inclined to look forward, rather than backwards, and we happily forget how often projects run over, things cost more than budgeted, or sales orders fall through. We're also likely to forget how our competitors behave — for example, getting excited about new opportunities while simultaneously disregarding the likelihood of our competitors doing exactly the same thing.

So, how do you avoid falling foul of the planning fallacy? Similar to avoiding confirmation bias, try to involve multiple perspectives and get input from experts or external advisors of the challenges or time required. In addition, you may be able to refer to past projects or industry benchmarks to guide your estimates, rather than relying solely on gut feeling. (For more about benchmarks, see Chapter 10.)

The Dunning-Kruger effect

Humans also tend to be optimistic in their struggle to make sense of the future and its mix of certainty and uncertainty. Or, put another way, because we don't yet know what we do not know, we tend to overestimate ourselves. This overestimation of competence, along with the inability to critically analyze our own abilities, is known as the *Dunning–Kruger effect*.

I've observed the Dunning–Kruger effect in action more times than I care to mention and, indeed, can see how often I've overestimated my own abilities. I've been influenced by life experiences that have been ultimately quite misleading, and sometimes my intuition and business decisions have been quite unhinged from reality.

WARNING

If you're new to business, or to a particular industry, beware of the risk that you could overrate yourself and underrate others who are more experienced. While self-confidence is essential, knowledge and rational decision-making processes are key to tethering your dreams. Instead, try to surround yourself with people who know a lot about the subject, particularly if the financial or legal stakes are high. Also, if you can, try to expand your knowledge by any means you can, be this through online courses, specialist training, or business coaching.

Understanding unconscious bias

Unconscious biases that affect our business judgment don't only relate to over-optimism. Consider some other patterns of behavior, and how these might affect the way you approach your business plan:

>> **Action-oriented bias:** An action-oriented bias is the tendency for people to move to action-oriented discussions too soon during the strategic planning process. I find this bias often comes from time pressures, or simply a lack of systematic thinking skills.

If you're making a significant decision, one trick to avoid action-orientated bias is to spend almost as much time justifying what you're not going to do as you spend justifying what you are going to do. For example, if you were to decide to purchase a factory, you might spend just as much time exploring what it would mean to lease instead, or even to outsource production.

» **Anchor bias and the primacy effect:** An anchor bias is about depending too much on initial information (the anchor) to make subsequent judgments, and not taking time to evaluate other strategic alternatives objectively. Similar is the primacy effect, which is the tendency to consider the first information you encounter more than later information.

One of the main ways to guard against anchor bias and the primacy effect is to slow down. Doing business plans can be hard work, and you may be tempted to hurry through certain stages. Pause regularly and ask yourself whether you've genuinely taken enough time to consider all your options. Sometimes, just an hour or two of objectively considering all your alternatives can prevent you spending months or even years pursuing a subpar business model.

» **Framing effect:** The framing effect is about we respond to the way information is framed. For example, if a business proposal is framed as cutting costs to prevent losses, this may seem more attractive than investing in growth despite risks.

To avoid the framing effect, always be aware about how strategic alternatives are framed. Try to reframe positive suggestions in a negative light, and vice versa, to see how that makes you feel. Alternatively, seek out external expert advice to evaluate alternatives, and ask for fresh opinions.

Finding Life Hacks to Help Do the Job

I'd love to know how many people reading this chapter will actually go on to complete a business plan. Far be it from me to express doubt about you, dear reader, or indeed about my own abilities to write a coherent tome on this topic, but my experience is that for every ten people who intend to create a proper business plan, only one or two do.

If you think you too may find it hard to complete the whole business plan shindig, here are a few life hacks to help:

» **Don't rely on your own willpower.** Instead, make planning into a habit, allocating a specific half-day per month, or a specific hour per week. Block out this time on your calendar.

» **Subscribe to a business-planning app.** I talk about apps earlier in this chapter (refer to 'Subscribing to a planning app'). Most apps make the planning process a little easier to navigate and more fun. And, for some, that monthly debit for the app subscription may prove motivation in itself.

TIP

» **Break the planning process into small steps.** Set small, actionable goals for each part of the business plan process — for example, completing a marketing plan one week, a pricing strategy review the next, and setting up financial templates the next.

» **Trick yourself into making the plan feel urgent.** Perhaps set a deadline to meet with an investor, nominate your business for an award, or schedule planning meetings with staff for which you need to prepare materials.

» **Find an accountability buddy.** Like finding a gym partner, find a friend or colleague who also needs to create a plan for their business, and agree to keep each other on track.

» **Spend time actively visualizing the future for your business (and you).** By making the future seem more real, you can sometimes motivate yourself into acting now.

TIP

You may be wondering why I spend so much time in the very first chapter of this book talking about how the psychology of the average human is not ideal for business planning. After all, might it not be better if I was a bit more encouraging? My hope is if you do end up finding the process a little daunting, you can take comfort from knowing that the problem isn't personal. And, with a little understanding about the psychology of the process, you can embark on your business plan with a greater chance of success.

Good luck, dear reader!

WHEN A SIDE HUSTLE SHOULD REMAIN JUST THAT

When is a successful side hustle an indicator of the perfect business idea, and when should a side hustle remain just that?

I suggest you ask yourself two questions. Firstly, will you have enough demand for your product or service if you expand what you're doing five- or tenfold? For example, perhaps you have a side hustle selling products at local markets. If you seek to expand your business, you probably need to look for new channels to sell your product, and the cost of reaching additional customers (for example, renting a retail space or selling products through a distributor) may skew your business model and make it less profitable.

Secondly, do you properly cost the value of your own labor? Perhaps, for example, you make homemade jams and pickles and you find time to do the manufacture around your day-to-day life, perhaps making batches of produce in the evenings or on weekends. If you turn this side hustle into your main hustle and you need to value your time (or, indeed, the time of others) at a decent hourly rate, can your pricing model sustain this adjustment?

Chapter **2**

Figuring Out What's So Special about You

What is it that makes you, or your business, so special?

Even if you have a business that's similar to thousands of others — maybe you mow lawns, have a hair salon, or tutor high-school students — if you wish to make above-average profits, you still need to come up with an idea that makes your business different from others, or that provides you with a competitive edge.

Similarly, if your business caters for a very specific niche — maybe you sell gluten-free cookies or baby clothes made from organic cottons — to make above-average profits, you need to identify how you can service this niche in a way that others can't, or what it is about your skills or circumstances that enables you to service this niche better than others.

If your business centers on an idea that you reckon nobody has tried before, the million-dollar question is why nobody else has bothered to try this idea until now. In the event that you're successful, the next key question is what prevents others from copying your idea straightaway.

The essence of what makes your business special, or more likely to succeed than others, is called your *competitive* or *strategic advantage*. I believe that this advantage is the single most important ingredient for ongoing business success, and is elemental to how you frame your business plan.

In this chapter, I outline how to determine your edge, and how to include your strategic advantage in your business plan.

Understanding Strategic Advantage

In the introduction for this chapter, I mention the terms *competitive advantage* and *strategic advantage*. These two terms tend to overlap so much that I try to avoid getting bogged down in arguing about the distinction. I use the term strategic advantage in this chapter (because, after all, a true strategic advantage should ultimately result in a competitive advantage) but if you'd rather use the term competitive advantage in your business plan, that's just fine.

Gaining the edge

How can your business beat the competition, and what benefits can you provide that the competition can't? Here are some ways that your business may be able to secure a strategic advantage against others in the same industry:

TIP

>> **Added value:** Can you offer added value in comparison to your competitors? Think 24-hour delivery, ethically sourced product, a mobile service, or a quality of product or service that's beyond industry norms.

>> **Excellent location:** If you have a retail shopfront, do you have a great location in a central shopping area? (Location is always the prime strategic advantage for retailers.) Or are you the only business providing a service in a particular suburb or region? Are the demographics of your location ideally matched to your business, or are you located in a central spot for freight and transport?

>> **Exclusive distribution rights:** Do you have exclusive distribution rights to a sought-after product or service?

>> **First cab off the rank:** Do you have a new idea that nobody else has tried before? Or a new way of doing something that makes the product or service better, quicker, or cheaper?

>> **Intellectual property:** Do you have unique intellectual property (IP) that customers want and that's hard to copy? IP includes copyright, patents, and trademarks. If you're just getting started with your business, your IP could be as simple as a clever business name, an eye-catching logo, or a well-chosen domain name (that is, a web address).

>> **Lower costs:** Do you have an innovative way of doing things that reduces costs, creates economies of scale, or significantly improves business processes?

>> **Obsession and drive:** Do you have exceptional vision or drive? Is this drive connected with a particular obsession? (For example, think of Coco Chanel with her ambitious vision and flair for design.)

>> **Perfectly matched team:** If you're in a business partnership of some kind, do you have a unique combination of skills and do you work well together as a team? (The synergy created by two or more people who have complementary skills and who work well together can be a force to be reckoned with, and something that's hard for competition to copy.)

>> **Specialist skills:** Are you a specialist who has an insight into a particular industry that nobody else is likely to have? Maybe you can see a gap in the industry that nobody else is catering for, or maybe you can see a way to do something better.

TIP

Think of a business that has been really successful (maybe a local business or a friend's business, or even a big name such as IKEA, Patagonia, or Microsoft). Go through the strategic advantages listed here, and think about which of these advantages could apply to these businesses.

From here, think about how you can find a strategic advantage for your own business. What can you do better than anybody else?

Avoiding the trap of being the cheapest

WARNING

When looking for a strategic advantage for your own business, don't fall into the trap of thinking that because you're cheaper than everyone else, this is a strategic advantage. Being cheaper than everyone else usually means one of two things: Either your business isn't as profitable as it should be, or your competitors can grab your strategic advantage at any moment just by dropping their prices too. Usually, being cheaper than others is only a strategic advantage if you have some special skills, technology, or volume of production that enables you to be cheaper.

Trading risk and gain

In most situations, the business with the highest potential strategic advantage is going to be the business that requires the most capital or involves the highest risk of failure. For example, imagine you had a really creative idea for a new fitness app. Your idea potentially has great strategic advantage (a new invention or first cab off the rank), but is almost certainly quite risky. (Smartphone apps generally have high development costs, an unknown and untested market, and may not even work that well when complete.)

In contrast, a safe business, such as lawn mowing, has few potential strategic advantages but involves the lowest risk of all. (The cost to set up this business could be as low as a few business cards.) Strategic advantages are hard to find for this kind of business because a lawn is only ever a lawn, and the owner will be limited in what to offer that others can't.

REMEMBER

Identifying potential strategic advantages for a business or service that lots of other people provide, and where it's difficult to differentiate between your service and those of your competitors, can be tricky. The upside of this kind of business is that the risks are usually lower; the downside is that it's always going to be tricky to charge premium rates or make above-average profits.

Justifying why you can succeed

For a strategic advantage to be really worth something — in terms of the goodwill of your business or your likely financial success — this advantage has to be something that you can sustain over the long term.

I like to think that any really strong strategic advantage should have three attributes:

>> **The advantage can't be easily copied by others.** The ideal strategic advantage is one that's really tricky for your competition to copy. Examples are a winning recipe or flavor (think Coca-Cola), a unique synergy of skills within your organization, or expert knowledge that few others have.

>> **The advantage is important to customers.** Think of the farmers who switched to growing organic produce in the early 1990s, before organics became more mainstream. Many of these farmers did really well because organics were so important to particular customers. (And although the advantage was relatively easy to copy, many authorities required a seven-year lead time with no chemicals before a farm could be officially certified.)

>> **The advantage can be constantly improved.** If you can identify the thing that gives you an edge and constantly work this advantage, you have a strategic advantage that is potentially sustainable in the long term.

TRUE
STORY

When Steve Jobs and Steve Wozniak started Apple, one key strategic advantage was that they were a perfectly matched team, and were passionate about design. The synergy of their skills was hard for others to copy, the beautiful design was something that customers really wanted, and Apple were in a position to continually improve and develop this advantage.

Developing Your Strategic Advantage Statement

In this book, I'm realistic about the written part of business plans. I know how few people actually write a 20- or 30-page business plan, despite their best intentions (which is why I also cover creating pitch decks and one-page business plans in Chapter 12).

However, even if you put nothing else in writing, I do recommend you write a statement of strategic advantage. In this statement, your purpose is to articulate exactly what gives your business an edge over others.

Your strategic advantage statement is usually similar but slightly different from your 'elevator speech'. The difference is that a strategic advantage statement may include information about your business that you wouldn't necessarily share if 'giving the sell' about your business to a prospective customer.

Note that if you are writing a full business plan, your strategic advantage statement forms part of your Executive Summary. (For more about Executive Summaries, see Chapter 12.)

Focusing on where you have the edge

Your strategic advantage statement needs only be a paragraph or two, but should include the following:

>> Your company name

>> How your product or service benefits your customers

>> What makes your business different from your competitors, seen from the perspective of your customers

>> Your strategic advantage or advantages: What knowledge, skills, synergy, team, technology, or processes your business has that enables you to deliver these additional benefits to your customers

I like to put this statement right at the beginning of any business plan because this insight into how you're different, and how you can succeed where others may fail or flounder, is so foundational to success.

Figure 2-1 shows an example of an extract from Dave's business plan (making homes toddler-proof).

Baby Busters provides a one-stop shop to help parents create a safe home. We not only assess the home for dangers, but also provide the required products and install them properly.

No other businesses within a two-hour radius provide a similar service. We are different from competitors in that our installer (Dave) is not only a licensed carpenter, but also trained in occupational health and safety and has worked as a Risk Assessment Officer. Alex has a marketing degree and currently works in real estate, which brings a special advantage in that he knows when people are moving into new homes and most likely to require this service.

FIGURE 2-1: An example statement of strategic advantage.

In Figure 2-1, Dave and his business partner, Alex, stress how the synergy of their skills and current occupations form their main strategic advantage. Some of these skills are also selling points for their business (for example, Dave's experience with risk assessment), but some are not (knowing when people are buying new homes so you can sell your product to them may be a strategic advantage, but it's definitely not a selling point).

Honing your difference over time

Sometimes your strategic advantage isn't something that's blindingly clear from the moment you set out in business, but instead grows over time. Your skills grow as you develop in business, and your understanding of how you're different from the competition consolidates as well.

From time to time, you can review your strategic advantage by asking yourself these questions:

>> What am I naturally good at? (Or what is my team good at?) Where do I feel I have been particularly successful in my business?

>> What do I offer to my customers that's cheaper than my competitors, better value, or unique in some way?

>> Does a point exist where what I'm naturally good at connects with what I do better than my competitors? If so, how can I build and develop this?

Using AI to Generate More Ideas

Whether you're still tossing around ideas for a new business or you've been running a business for years, keep an open mind about new ways of doing business. I find that an AI app such as ChatGPT can be useful for this purpose.

The trick with AI is phrasing your question in the right way. When using AI to explore different ways of doing business, be as specific as possible and try asking the same question in a few different ways:

>> **Ask AI to generate a list of successful companies in your industry.** While you may know which businesses are most

successful in the country where you live, have you checked out other businesses overseas? What might you learn by visiting the websites of those companies? For example, if you're thinking of starting an e-bike business, you might ask AI to 'list the most successful e-bike businesses in France', or 'list the best e-bike retailers in Singapore'.

» **Ask AI how you can make money from a particular business idea.** I was genuinely impressed with ChatGPT's response to the question, 'How do I make money from a business mowing lawns?' (Although I did chuckle at the absurd suggestion that I 'consider offering mobile services to mow lawns off-site'.) What comes up for you if you type into AI 'How do I make money from [insert your business idea here]?'

» **Ask AI how you might create a strategic advantage in a particular industry.** The question, 'How do I create a strategic advantage for a hair salon?' yielded some interesting results, as did, 'I'm a designer creating websites for medical professionals. How can I create a strategic advantage?'

» **Ask AI for suggestions about businesses doing things completely differently.** Writing questions that include both your industry or business model as well as the word 'disruptor' can lead to some interesting ideas.

TIP

When trying to generate ideas for how to gain strategic advantage, don't limit your research to the state or even the country in which you live. Go global with your online research, visiting websites of similar businesses all around the world. Consider how you might emulate good marketing strategy ideas, innovative pricing models, smart online services, or other clever approaches.

REMEMBER

Be prepared to revisit your ideas repeatedly and keep reshaping the concept that you have for your business until you can come up with a strong strategic advantage.

Chapter **3**

Sizing up the Competition

'm still surprised at how often I come across people planning to start a new business, or who are in the first couple of years of business, who have yet to research who their competitors are.

Detailed competitive analysis helps clarify what it is that your business is going to do better than others. As part of this analysis, I recommend organizing your competitors into groups, differentiating between 'head-on-head' competitors, and competitors who only take away business from you on an occasional basis. You also need to think about future competitors — competitors who aren't a big deal yet, but could become so if circumstances change.

In this chapter, I talk about doing a thorough profile for key competitors, picking apart the differences between them and your own business. I also return to the question: Given what the competition are doing and how they are faring, how does this reflect on how your business is likely to perform?

Understanding Why Competitor Analysis is Important

Business planning can be a dry topic at the best of times, and you may already feel that you have a handle on who your competitors are. However, thinking about your competitors in detail is important for three key reasons: First, as a reality check; second, for spotting opportunities; third, as a way to figure out how you're going to stand out from the pack.

Avoiding blind faith

Part of the excitement of starting a new business is the buzz you get when coming up with new ideas. However, the trick is to know when confidence crosses the line to become blind faith.

Checking out potential competitors thoroughly is one way of getting a reality check. For example, in a town near me, a whole strip of cafés come and go with every change in season. If I were thinking about starting a café in this town, a competitor analysis may well reveal that the rents in this strip are high, the landlords difficult, and nobody is making enough profits to survive, let alone thrive.

Similarly, without competitor analysis, you can't be sure of your financial modelling. If you have direct competitors, you want to be right across the services these businesses provide, and the prices they charge. Unless a massive undersupply exists or you're offering a valuable difference, charging significantly more for your product or your service than your competitors may prove to be a highly risky business model; similarly, undercutting competitors on price is unlikely to be viable.

Spotting potential opportunities

Your competition isn't just the marker of who you have to 'beat'. Your competition can also be a source of inspiration or the benchmark that enables you to establish realistic expectations for your business, and provide insight into where you can gain a possible edge.

Buying goods or services from your competitors (as opposed to just researching them online) can be a great way to reveal potential opportunities. Indeed, the seed of many a winning business idea is sown by someone receiving poor service or a disappointing product. Whenever you think, *I can do better than that*, the potential for a new business idea or marketing strategy is born.

Of course, you may well find that your competitors have some pretty good ideas you could potentially adapt for your business. Pricing specials, weekend packages, discount offers, online services, creative advertising, or clever sales techniques are just some of the things you may decide to explore. After all, imitation is the greatest form of flattery (although your competitors may not see it that way!).

REMEMBER

Always look for differences other than price when comparing yourself against competitors. Keep asking yourself what makes you special and how you intend to convey this difference clearly in your marketing materials. Unless you know exactly what your competitors provide, you won't know how to sell your differences.

Assessing Your Competitors

You can't create a battle plan without knowing the enemy. In the following sections, I explore how to figure out who the enemy really is (otherwise known as your competitors, of course) and how to create a battle plan for each act of combat.

TIP

When doing your competitor analysis, don't hesitate to compare your business against big-time competitors such as supermarket chains or large franchises. While you may find it hard to imagine how your fledgling business could ever compete, the mass-market nature of these competitors often leaves niches that are underserved, providing opportunities for smaller players.

Organizing competitors into groups

I like to organize competitors into three broad groups, and I suggest you try to do so too, as follows:

>> **Head-to-head competitors** provide exactly the same service or exactly the same product as you do.

>> **'Sometimes' competitors** provide a slightly different service or product, or are in a different location.

>> **Left-field competitors** don't normally compete with you but, if circumstances were to change, could possibly do so.

Imagine you're a digital marketing agency specializing in brand development. Your head-to-head competitors are likely other digital agencies with this same focus working in your region or state; your 'sometimes' competitors could include freelance copywriters operating from anywhere in the world; your left-field competition might include an AI tool designed to generate creative copy.

In the same way, if you're an osteopath specializing in back pain, your head-to-head competitors would include other osteopaths providing exactly the same service in the same area; your 'sometimes' competitors could include allied health practitioners such as physiotherapists; left-field competition could include prescription pain killers.

Although figuring out current competitors may sound relatively easy, future competitors are not always so easy to spot. For example, a watchmaker repairing and selling watches 40 years ago would have probably thought that the main competition was other watchmakers. The idea that the mobile phone could almost completely annihilate this industry would have seemed a long shot.

When you're thinking about the competition for your proposed business, don't be too literal — think about where both your business and its industry are headed.

Homing in on head-to-head competitors

For most businesses, the priority is to spend time analyzing head-to-head competitors. After all, these are the competitors that your customers are most often going to come across when they seek to purchase your goods or services.

One of the purposes of identifying head-to-head competitors is so you can develop a competitive strategy to deal with each one (refer to the section 'Understanding Why Competitor Analysis is Important', earlier in this chapter, for more reasons). However, when you create a list of head-to-head competitors, this can sometimes be a long list.

For example, if you're starting up a business installing solar panels, you may find 50 other companies working in your local area offering similar services. You don't want to have to come up with 50 different competitive strategies, so your best tactic is to try to group these competitors in some way.

Try this process:

1. **List your competitors in a small number of groups based on similarities.**

    For example, a solar panel company may split its list of 50 similar companies according to the size of each business, and focus (maybe some focus on battery storage, others on off-grid, others on new buildings), or by locality or suburb.

2. **Think about how you've organized these groups. Will a customer looking for your kind of business use these same criteria?**

    For example, if a customer is searching online for a solar panel company, are they going to search by suburb, by specialty, or by services provided?

3. **Have a think about where you belong in the scheme of things.**

    The solar panel company may decide to focus on solar systems but within a two-hour travel radius only.

4. **Think to the future. Do you want to be in this same group in five years' time?**

    For example, maybe the solar panel company has a vision that ultimately they want to offer not just solar installations, but home-energy consultations also, and they want to expand to offer this service nationwide.

TIP

By organizing your competitors into groups, you can build a clearer idea about how to develop different competitive strategies, depending on what kind of competitor you're dealing with.

Thinking about future competitors

In Chapter 5, I talk about your vision for the future, and how important it is to keep your eyes open to trends in the economy, the environment, and in your industry. This macro way of thinking is also useful at the early planning stages of your business, particularly if you spend a while thinking about not just who your competitors are right now, but also who your competitors could be in one, two, or five years' time.

Ask yourself questions relating to the following areas:

- » **Automation potential:** Could any existing competitors automate their processes using advanced technology and, therefore, become more of a threat than they already are?

- » **Big chains coming to town:** Could a franchise chain or large company move into your village, suburb, or town and take lots of your customers? (In my neighborhood, the longstanding boutique wine store was greatly impacted when two big liquor chains moved into the same neighborhood.)

- » **Buyout of minor competitors by a larger competitor with more capital and muscle:** Could one of your existing competitors be bought out by someone with more capital and better distribution and, in the process, become a very formidable competitor? (Think about how some producers of gourmet food products have been purchased by supermarket chains and the products suddenly appear in every store.)

- » **Changes in technology:** Could changes in technology mean your product or service becomes obsolete? (Think of the long-lost corner video store, the TV repairer, or the 24-hour photo lab.)

- » **Cheaper imports:** Could the goods you provide be substituted by imported goods if the exchange rate changes?

- » **Customers doing it themselves:** Could your main customer or customers decide creating your product or providing your service in-house makes more sense? (Think of the supermarket chains that now manufacture their own generic food lines.)

- » **Life cycle of business idea:** Is the life cycle of your business reaching maturity or beyond, meaning numerous competitors and fewer profits to go around? (Think of the mobile coffee vans that were once a clever niche business but are now a dime a dozen.)

- » **Offshoring of labor:** Could the services you provide be performed offshore instead? (Almost anything that's mostly labor and can be done online is vulnerable to offshoring.)

>> **Service offered online:** Could the service you provide be sold online and, therefore, open to international competition? (Even some things that I would never have imagined could go online have done so. I don't go to my local yoga class any more, but instead log onto a yoga website that offers hundreds of pre-recorded classes to fit any duration, level, or style of yoga.)

Mirror, mirror on the wall . . .

Who's the fairest of them all?

One thing to remember when you compare yourself against others is that you don't need to be perfect, offer rock-bottom pricing or, provide unbelievable service and availability. Instead, all you need to be is that little bit better than your competitor.

For example, imagine a physiotherapist starting up in a new town has decided they want to offer an after-hours service. They discover that the only competitor offering an after-hours service is still only available until 6.30 pm on weekdays. In order to be competitive for an after-hours service, this physiotherapist doesn't need to be available 24/7 — staying open until 8 pm will do just fine, and will meet the needs for those customers hunting around for someone after hours.

Of course, opening hours aren't the only variable that you need to consider, and Table 3-1 shows a detailed competitive analysis of how this physiotherapist compares with others in the local area, rating competitors according to what they do better (or worse).

TABLE 3-1   Rating Head-to-Head Competitors

Does this competitor . . .	Move Plus	Physio Now	Injury+	JPS
Have cheaper pricing than me?	Yes	No	No	No
Offer longer opening hours or availability?	No	No	Yes	Yes
Offer specific services that I don't?	No	Yes	No	Yes
Have better distribution or service a wider region?	No	No	No	Yes

(continued)

TABLE 3-1 *(continued)*

Does this competitor . . .	Move Plus	Physio Now	Injury+	JPS
Offer a larger variety of pricing packages?	No	No	Yes	Yes
Have more expertise/higher level of skill/higher qualifications?	No	No	No	Yes
Service all the niches that I service?	No	No	No	No
Have respect and trust in the community?	Yes	No	No	Yes
Have an active social media presence?	No	No	Yes	Yes
Have a good online marketing strategy?	No	No	Yes	Yes
Have more capital and power to expand?	No	No	Yes	Yes

When you do this competitive analysis for your own business, you may want to insert additional criteria against which to compare yourself, or include more than four competitors in your analysis. The important thing is that you list your comparison criteria in the first column, and the names of the competitors that you're comparing yourself along the top. Below each competitor, write yes if they're better and no if you're better (or not applicable if this isn't relevant to you).

For head-to-head competitors, I suggest that you also document their pricing strategies, who their target market seems to be, how many employees they have, and whether they seem to be struggling or thriving. Check out your competitors' marketing materials, website and online reviews, in particular.

Choosing Your Competitive Strategy

So, what next? You've listed all of your competitors, organized them into groups, checked out how they're going, and compared all the main competitors against yourself. (And, if you haven't done these things, head to the start of this chapter and read through.) The next step is to choose your competitive strategy.

Going for cheapest, different, or niche

Any business is faced with these three possible competitive strategies: *Cost leadership*, *differentiation*, or *niche*. You may choose only one of the strategies, you could choose two, or you may choose a combination of all three:

>> **You can choose to be the cheapest (cost leadership strategy).** With this strategy, you're not necessarily the cheapest across all products you offer or the cheapest for every service but, in general, you're aiming to compete on price. Price leadership can be a tempting strategy — after all, customers are always looking for a bargain — but is risky over the long term. Unless you have a strategic advantage that enables you to deliver your product or service more cheaply than your competitors, competing on price can mean weak profitability, and a business model that is doomed to underperform from the get-go.

>> **You can set out to create a point of difference (differentiation strategy).** With this strategy, you set out to differentiate yourself from similar competitors. For example, an electrician could seek to make response time and punctuality a point of difference ('We'll arrive within 30 minutes of the agreed time or the first hour is free'), or could make availability a point of difference ('24-hour call-out service, 7 days a week').

Ideally, if you choose differentiation as your competitive strategy, you want to find a synergy between this differentiation and your strategic advantage (for more about strategic advantage, refer to Chapter 2). To illustrate this, let's return to the physiotherapist example. Maybe a strategic advantage for this physiotherapist is that they are also an elite athlete, and have several strong partnerships with sports coaches. By selecting a differentiation strategy and focusing on expertise treating sports injuries, they combine their strategic advantage with their competitive strategy.

>> **You can find a particular focus or niche (niche strategy).** With this strategy, your aim is to serve a specific market segment rather than dealing with the whole market.

You can combine this niche strategy with a cost strategy, of course (by focusing on one specific niche, you may end up being the cheapest), and you can certainly combine a niche strategy with a differentiation strategy (because the differentiation itself becomes a niche). In a market where niche products or services are increasingly discoverable online and people are seeking bespoke choices more than ever, this competitive strategy is increasingly viable for many businesses.

REMEMBER

You can choose cost leadership or differentiation as competitive strategies in their own right. However, if you choose a niche strategy, implicit in that is that you're also choosing a differentiation strategy. (In other words, you can choose differentiation as your competitive strategy without having a niche, but by its very nature choosing a niche as your competitive strategy means that you're also choosing to differentiate.)

Pulling the pin, if need be

What should you do if you can't identify a clear strategic advantage or competitive strategy? I don't want to be too harsh, but if you can't figure out what you're going to do differently, and why, then perhaps your business model is a weak one.

In this situation, what becomes relevant is measuring up the risks. If starting (or continuing with) this business means little capital outlay and a few lost weekends and holidays, you probably don't have much to lose. On the other hand, if this business involves your retirement savings and/or the threat of a failed relationship if things go wrong, the risk may be unjustifiable.

REMEMBER

However much you want to believe in your business idea, if a high level of risk is involved (either personally or financially), do weigh this risk against the likely strength of your business model. Remember that part of the rationale of creating a business plan is to identify weaknesses in your ideas. And, if this means that you pull the pin on a business before it has even begun, that's the very definition of a successful business plan.

Chapter **4**

Separating Yourself from Your Business

M any years ago, I did some consulting work for a guy who'd started his own industrial welding business. The reporting systems for this business were a complete nightmare. As I trawled through the accounts, trying to make sense of it all, my client looked across the room at me and announced, in a somewhat apologetic tone, 'You know something? I'm a really good welder'.

For me, this brief interchange summarizes the dilemma many business owners face. People start out in their business doing what they're good at, and what they love to do (whether this is welding, performing music, or face-painting at kids' parties). But before long, they find they spend more and more time doing stuff they're not naturally good at, such as bookkeeping, looking through contracts, hiring employees, or managing websites. Sometimes this extra work becomes such a burden that the joy of being in business is lost. Or sometimes the business owner rises to the challenge, thriving on these extra demands and enjoying the reprieve from day-to-day tasks.

In this chapter, I explore the questions that get to the heart of what you want to achieve with your business. Do you plan to take on employees and grow your business? Do you have a unique concept that means you could potentially sell your business for a substantial profit in five or ten years' time? Or are you happy tinkering away in your home office, earning a modest income with little stress and few demands?

No answer is right, no answer is wrong. However, the process of creating a business plan provides an ideal opportunity for you to decide the direction in which you wish to head.

Deciding What Path You Want to Take

Generally, business-planning books assume that you want to grow your business, take on employees, maybe even develop a franchise or expand internationally. (After all, the very expression 'business planning' implies an intention to expand and develop.)

However, in the first part of this chapter, I want to spend a bit of time exploring whether you feel this desire for expansion. Maybe you're quite content pursuing a small home-based part-time business, or maybe you don't want the stress of taking on employees.

Taking a step back and thinking of all the businesspeople I know or have worked with, I can see that most people follow one of three paths (or occasionally all three paths, but one after the other):

>> A simple owner-operated business with no employees.

>> A business where the owner focuses on providing the service but employs others to help run administrative functions of the business.

>> A business founded by the owner that then has a life of its own, where employees deliver services or manufacture products, and the owner is in a management role as a company director. Ultimately, the business expands to operate independently of its original founder.

Which path do you want to take? Even though most business books imply that if you're serious about being in business, the third path is the only way forward, this isn't necessarily true. Small owner-operated businesses may have less opportunity for profit, but profit is only one of the many motivators for being in business.

Doing the thing you love to do

Most people start a business doing the thing that they have experience doing, or possibly the thing that they've just completed studying. So the person who was working as a high-school teacher starts a business tutoring high-school students, the physiotherapist who was working at her local hospital opens her own practice, or the qualified chef opens a restaurant.

The upside of running a business in this way is that you get to do what you love to do, and usually what you're good at. You also have the perks of self-employment (choosing your own hours, possibly charging more for your services, and being your own boss).

REMEMBER

The downside of being a solo owner-operator is often long hours, with no income when you're on holidays or if you're sick. The experience of being cleaner, shop assistant, bookkeeper, marketing manager, and finance manager all within the course of a single day can be relentless, and you may end up feeling that you're a jack-of-all-trades but a master of none. Your business is utterly dependent on you; if you don't turn up, you don't get paid. In addition, the amount of money you can make from your business is always limited by the number of hours you're able to work.

Some people would argue that the kind of work involved with an owner-operator business, where it's just you and you do your own thing, defeats the purpose of going into business. They would argue that unless you want to conceive of a business that has a life of its own beyond yourself, you're better just to keep working for someone else. Otherwise, you're not really creating a business; rather, you're creating a job with a pile of overheads.

I disagree. Although I acknowledge that this small-scale kind of operation has its drawbacks, I've lived in a regional area and been self-employed for too long to be that naïve. Sometimes no jobs are available and the only option is to be self-employed. Sometimes you may have such substantial family commitments that your business becomes a relatively peripheral part of your life, and the income it generates is just a bonus, not the core.

Sometimes the way you generate income is so personal, so idio-syncratic (maybe you're an artist, a faith healer, or an inventor) that you can't conceive of a way that this business can be grown beyond yourself. All of these reasons are perfectly valid reasons for being in business, yet staying small.

So, having explored the pros and cons, what is my advice for people who are currently self-employed with no employees (or planning to start a new business with this structure)? If you have valid reasons for staying as an owner-operator, and don't want to expand, then that's okay. However, if you haven't yet spent time thinking of ways to grow your business so that it's not entirely dependent on your labor, I recommend you take the time to do so.

Conceiving a way to run your business so that it can operate with-out you can be challenging, but is the only way forward if you want to generate profits that aren't directly dependent on the hours that you work — which, incidentally, is what the rest of this chapter is all about.

Getting help and delegating what you can

If you're not content to be an owner-operator doing everything yourself, the first and most natural stage of expansion is usually to employ some assistance. Maybe you hire a bookkeeper, employ a casual laborer or contractor, or get assistance with marketing or website design.

Many experts and professionals end up with this kind of model. For example, our local orthodontist hires several employees (two receptionists, a dental hygienist, and an office manager) but she is the only person delivering the specialist service on which the business depends. Sure, she could probably hire another ortho-dontist to work for her, but she has a great deal invested in her reputation and, for whatever reason, feels she can't trust another person to provide the same quality of service.

In a way, the part of my business income that I generate writing books is similar. I employ a bookkeeper and office admin person, and occasionally get help researching topics, but at the end of day (and I confess that it's truly the end of the day as I write this), the only ones left standing are me and my little silver laptop.

This way of working is what many people choose. You get to do the thing you love and you can choose your own hours, be your own boss, and usually make a decent living. And, unlike single owner-operators who do everything themselves, you can hire others to help with day-to-day business operations, so that you can focus on doing the thing that you're good at.

The downside, of course, is that you're still 'it' as far as the business is concerned. You are your business, and your business is you. Your income is always limited by the number of hours you're able to work, and if you're on holiday or sick, the business doesn't generate income.

If your business has this kind of structure, you may find it hard to imagine how you can expand your business so that employees could provide the same services as you currently do. However, nobody is indispensable, and no matter how smart or talented you are, chances are someone's out there who can do all the things you do.

TIP

One of the tricks to making the leap to hiring others to provide the services you currently provide is to imagine a little person is sitting on your shoulder, watching everything you do and documenting your activities in a 'how-to' manual. This is the first step towards separating yourself from your business, so that you can describe to others the attitudes, skills and standards that you expect. (For more on this topic, see the section 'Creating systems', later in this chapter.)

Building a business that's separate from you

The third path that you can take (refer to the preceding sections for an outline of the other two paths) is to create a business where employees are the ones providing your service or manufacturing your products. To work in this way, you need to find a business model where the service or product sold is not reliant on your continuous input.

If you look around you, most medium-sized businesses fall into this category. For example:

>> A digital media agency employs a team of specialists to deliver their services; the two company directors who set up

the agency now focus primarily on staffing and customer acquisition.

>> A music school has several tutors teaching different instruments, with studios in several locations. The founders of the school focus on branding, systems, and expansion, and rarely deliver one-on-one music lessons to students.

>> A sourdough bakery that started as a home-based project during the pandemic now has outlets all around the state. These days, the two friends who started this business focus on staffing, quality control, distribution, and supply chain management; neither misses the pre-dawn starts involved in baking bread themselves.

>> A supplier of customizable sleeping bags for babies, which started as a home-based business, now has offshore production, a sales distributor, and a team of administration and marketing staff.

Can you see that for each of these examples, the business owners have made a leap in how they think of their businesses? The digital media consultant is now the manager of a digital agency; the music tutors started their own music school; the bakers opened a chain of bakeries; the craftsperson runs a manufacturing company. In all of these examples, the owner no longer writes copy, teaches violin, bakes bread, or stitches fabric. In return, the potential for each of these businesses is that the owners can have more freedom and earn more money than they otherwise would have done.

For me, this transition from owner to entrepreneur is really exciting. Freedom from the shackles of the daily grind provides an opportunity to do the other things in life that have only been dreams up until now.

If you haven't made this transition, and your business is still dependent on you for pretty much every cent of income, my question to you is this: Have you ever consciously made the decision not to be entrepreneurial? Or have you never really let yourself imagine how you could do things differently?

If not, do try to give the visionary in you some room to breathe. Spend time thinking about how you can grow your business and create something that has a life of its own.

Creating a new way of doing business

The queen diva of all business models is, of course, the franchise. A franchise is where you figure out such a neat and unique way of doing business that this concept itself becomes something you can sell. A franchise embodies the whole way you do business, including buying policies, logos, marketing techniques, pricing, and uniforms. Table 4-1 outlines various business models, and how specific owner-operator businesses could move into the franchise or international model.

TABLE 4-1 **Moving from a Small Business to a Big Business**

Owner-Operator	Business with Employees	Franchise/ International Model
Yoga teacher	Yoga school	Patented method of teaching and streaming online yoga classes
Personal trainer	A gym with three employees	National franchise of fitness outlets
Online bookstore with national distribution	Online store selling books, electronics, and music with international distribution	An international e-commerce business spanning multiple industries, including logistics and delivery
A farmer selling homemade chili sauce and pickles	A chili sauce company with a recognized brand and national distribution	A method of manufacturing and distributing sauces/ pickles that can be replicated worldwide
A corner cafe in the local town	A couple of cafes with several employees	A franchise restaurant chain
A fashion blogger selling clothes online	An online clothing store with 50 brands and national distribution	An innovative system (including software) for selling clothes online that can be replicated in other countries
Your business	_____ (fill in the blanks)	_____ (fill in the blanks)

Note: I'm not talking about you purchasing a franchise here; rather, I'm talking about you building such a successful way of doing business that you create your own franchise.

Creating your own franchise takes the requirement that you separate yourself from your business to a whole new level. To use the example of the digital media company I refer to in the preceding section: When the company founders delegated consulting work to employees, they entrusted others to provide the core service of the business on their behalf and, to do this, they had to provide a certain level of supervision and training.

However, how could the owners take their business to the next level, and create a franchise that could operate in other countries or other industries? At this point, the founders would need to analyze what it is that makes their business different. They would need to quantify these differences and create systems so that others can copy these differences.

The upside of expanding to become a franchise is the opportunity to make very healthy profits. In many ways, a franchise is the ultimate realization of the entrepreneur's dream.

Wearing Different Hats

Have you heard of *The E-Myth* or *The E-Myth Revisited* (written by Michael Gerber and published by HarperBusiness)? This book, while a little dated now, sold over 3 million copies, and the terminology that Gerber used to describe the roles owners play in their businesses has become almost standard in some circles.

Gerber likes to describe the roles of a business owner as being technician, manager, or entrepreneur. I may not describe these roles here exactly as Gerber might, but here's the general idea:

>> **Technician:** These are people who work in their business, not on their business — the plumber who unblocks drains, the café owner who serves coffee, or the freelance consultant who goes out to meet clients.

>> **Manager:** A manager is someone who organizes the day-to-day running of a business, ordering stock, looking at profit margins, paying the bills and replying to customers.

>> **Entrepreneur:** An entrepreneur is the visionary, the person who's thinking of the business as a thing that's separate to the service it provides or the product it sells, and who is looking for ways to build the business and expand.

I really like this way of thinking of the roles in a business, because it goes a long way to explaining that feeling I've felt so often as a business owner, of having all these balls in the air that I have to juggle. The idea is that if it's just you in your business (which it is for most people when they start out), you need to balance out these roles. The idea sounds simple, but is tricky to do.

These roles correspond to some degree with what I talk about earlier in this chapter. Someone who is happiest being a 'technician' often ends up not expanding their business, and instead typically provides services or makes products themselves (refer to 'Doing the thing you love to do', earlier in this chapter). A person whose 'manager' side wins out typically ends up organizing others. This person is content to get employees to assist in running the business and is good at monitoring costs and ensuring efficient operations (refer to 'Getting help and delegating what you can'). The 'entrepreneur' personality is the one who's always looking for the winning idea, and is keenest to create a business with a life of its own (refer to 'Building a business that's separate from you' or 'Creating a new way of doing business').

WARNING

If your business is still pretty small, letting any one of the three roles of technician, manager, or entrepreneur dominate at the expense of the others can be a problem. The technician will probably fail to grow the business, the manager may well fail to look to the future and plan for change, and the entrepreneur, if left to their own devices, may burn through a whole load of money very quickly pursuing one idea after another.

What I think is so clever about the way Gerber identifies these roles is that you can apply this thinking to yourself and your own business. For example:

» Most people find that the technician role (doing the thing that they're good at, such as fixing pipes, teaching music or making a mean espresso coffee) feels comfortable and safe.

» The role of manager fits well with some people but not with others. (Many businesspeople hate having to think about money, tax, legals, schedules and so on, but others are relatively okay with this role.)

» The role of entrepreneur is the role that comes hardest to most people. If you're inherently a bit conservative (as I confess to being myself), whenever the entrepreneur voice pipes up with a good idea, your inner conservative manager voice likely calls out, 'Oh no, that's way too scary'. The entrepreneur and manager are so busy tussling away that the only person left to do anything is the technician, who continues to get on with the job. And then nothing changes.

The way to move on from this situation, and give all three roles a part to play, is to build a business that has a life of its own — which just happens to be the next topic in this chapter . . .

Building a Business with a Life of its Own

In the preceding sections in this chapter, I talk about why creating a business with a life of its own is generally the best way to gain more freedom and flexibility, and hopefully more profits to boot. I also talk about the different roles or 'hats' people typically wear in business, and how important it is to balance these roles, especially when you're just getting started and you have only you in the business.

However, the transition to creating a business with its own identity, separate from you, isn't always easy. In the following sections, I provide some guidelines as to how you may be able to make this happen.

Defining your difference

The first step in giving your business some of its own life force is to be clear about what it is that makes you different. I spend a heap of time deliberating on this very topic back in Chapter 2, so I won't repeat myself here. Suffice to say that you must identify what makes your business different, and this difference must relate to the identity of your business, and not you personally.

Some examples may help to set this in context:

>> A solar panel installer provides energy audits and a carbon footprint calculator as part of their service.

>> An online clothes store offers multiple views and videos of each item of clothing, and provides recommendations as to the body types each garment is best suited for.

>> A car repair shop offers a free home drop-off and pick-up service, and routinely details all vehicles as part of any service or repair work.

None of the preceding ideas is particularly revolutionary but, if executed well and combined with a cohesive marketing strategy and company commitment, they have the potential to make these businesses stand apart from others.

I find that business owners can be very vague regarding what it is that makes their business successful, especially with smaller businesses where the owner is still very much hands-on. To use the car repair shop example from the preceding list, this auto mechanic may offer free home drop-offs and detailing, but is this really the reason for the success of this business? Or is it that the head mechanic is such a lovely guy that customers instantly warm to him? Or that this is the only auto repair service within a 30-minute radius?

Without an understanding of what makes this business successful, the owner is vulnerable. If the drawcard is the head mechanic, what might happen to the business if he leaves? If the lack of competition in a 30-minute radius is the reason for steady business, what might happen if another auto mechanic opens up shop nearby?

You can try to deduce the reasons for your success using a few techniques:

>> If your business operates in more than one location, experiment by trialing specific services or marketing techniques in one location but not the other, and see what happens.

>> Return to the competitive analysis you did in Chapter 3 (or if you haven't already done it, do it now). This objective comparative process is a good way to get a sense of why your customers come to you.

>> Ask your customers why they love you! You can ask customers face to face, run surveys, put up quick questions on social media, or do whatever fits your customer base best.

>> Try opening a new location and trying to replicate your success from the first location. If the new location performs differently, try to get to the bottom of why.

>> If you think that part of your success is due to something relatively simple (I think of my local butcher who, after each interaction, looks at me with a smile and says, 'Can I get you anything else today?' — even if a queue of people is waiting behind me), then try measuring sales when you employ this technique or strategy for a week, and compare sales to another week where you don't do this.

If you can figure out why you're successful, and measure how much difference this strategy, product, or technique makes to your business, you're well on the way to being able to replicate your success and grow your business.

TIP

Creating systems

One of the things that a franchise offers, in contrast to other businesses of a similar type, is consistency. As a friend of mine likes to say in a satisfied voice regarding the coffee he buys from a certain fast-food chain, 'This bunch make the best worst coffee in the world'. In other words, he knows the coffee is going to be average, he knows it won't be that hot, but still it hits the spot and it's the same every time, wherever he is in the country.

This consistency is one of the secrets to expanding a business beyond one location, building a recognizable brand, or even preparing your business to become a franchise in its own right. Take the example of my aunt, who ran a guesthouse in the wilds of northern Scotland for 30 years or more. She was a wonderful hostess, but occasionally she'd be away for the weekend or even for a week or two. How could she guarantee that her guests would get exactly the same quality of experience when she was away as when she was there?

A happy customer may share the love with one or two people, but unhappy customers share their disgruntlement with ten. If you can get rid of the hit-and-miss element that plagues so many businesses, positive word-of-mouth recommendations may be almost all the marketing you need.

REMEMBER

So how do you guarantee consistency, particularly as your business grows and you're not around to serve each customer or supervise each employee? The answer lies in procedures and documentation. First, you figure out what it is that your business does well (which I cover in the preceding section); next, you articulate this difference in a way that employees can follow.

Here are some examples of how to provide a consistent experience for customers:

>> **Automations:** For any customer interactions that happen regularly (such as a customer signing up to a newsletter, purchasing a product, or making an enquiry), implement automations in your CRM (customer relationship management) software. Automations are simple sequences of emails or text messages that help you to provide a swift response, ensure quality customer service and secure customer engagement.

>> **Checklists:** For any complex activities, where employees need to fulfil several tasks in a specific sequence, create a checklist. For example, if your business is such that a customer order can be quite complex (maybe you need to check aspects such as quantities, availability, delivery dates and payment methods), a checklist ensures nothing gets forgotten.

REMEMBER

>> **Complaints procedures:** Do you know that one of the ways to make customers happiest is to do everything you can to fix something when they complain? However, the gentle art of responding well to a grumpy customer isn't something that comes naturally to most people, and so procedures for dealing with complaints are essential.

>> **Customer service procedures and processes:** Ideally, you need a procedure for any customer interaction that happens on a regular basis, whether this is a customer enquiry, order, or sale.

>> **Manufacturing procedures:** If you're a manufacturer, even if you're operating on a relatively small scale making things to sell locally or at markets, the quality of your product needs to be the same each time. Sounds simple, but imagine you're making homemade jams, and the quality of produce available varies according to the time of year. In this scenario, you may need to limit production to certain times of year in order to guarantee consistency.

Similarly, if you've been manufacturing products yourself and you're now ready to delegate this process, you need to document exactly what you do, using precise quantities, times, production methods and so on.

>> **Phone scripts and email templates:** I can feel you wincing a little here, as you wonder if you're really so dictatorial that you can bear writing out scripts for employees to follow when they answer the phone, or templates for when they reply to emails. Remember two things, however: First, what you're trying to achieve is consistency for the customer; second, if you have spent time figuring out the ingredients that have made your business successful and you know that how you answer the phone or reply to emails is part of this success, then, of course, you want to be able to repeat this formula, time and time again.

>> **Presentation:** As someone who hates uniform in almost any shape or form, I squirm a little as I write this. But businesses love uniforms for the reason that they provide consistency for the customer and reinforce the company's image. Even something as simple as a polo shirt with your company logo monogrammed on the front can make a difference to how customers perceive you.

>> **Rates and pricing:** Standardized rates and pricing are a must. So if you tend to quote on a somewhat intuitive basis for jobs, you need to spend time figuring out a method for pricing and stick to that instead.

TIP

If you're still small and you're thinking about how to expand your business, one great source of inspiration (if available) is to look at franchises that offer a similar service or product to your own. For example, if you're starting a lawnmowing business, take a look at how the lawnmowing franchises approach their branding, marketing and customer service. If you're starting a bookkeeping business, look at the bookkeeping franchises and how they organize their pricing and services. I'm not suggesting you steal intellectual property here or that you try to copy the systems of a franchise without paying to belong — more that you take a look at the general approach of this franchise and use this as inspiration. (Or, of course, you may even consider becoming a franchisee.)

Planning for a graceful exit

One of the best ways to get yourself into the mindset of thinking of your business as independent from you is to imagine selling it.

Always try to have an exit plan simmering away, even if you don't plan to sell any time in the immediate future. Ask yourself the following questions: If I were to sell this business today, what could I get for it? Can this business run independently of me? What assets or business systems do I have to sell? How can I maximize the price I can get for this business?

Appreciating the Limitations of Your Business

In the preceding sections in this chapter, I talk about the idea of creating a business that has a life of its own, separate from you. I also mention early in this chapter that not everyone wants to go down this path, and I talk about the pros and cons of operating your business in different ways.

When thinking on these topics, you also have to keep in mind that some businesses are much harder than others to expand. Here are some of the kinds of businesses that can be hard to grow, along with why:

>> **Businesses limited by physical constraints or high start-up costs that require substantial capital:** Farmers are an obvious example here, limited by the amount of land they have, and lacking capital to expand. Other examples could be a professional truck driver limited by the high capital cost of additional trucks, or the capacity of a guesthouse owner to expand due to the high cost of purchasing real estate.

>> **Businesses based on the artistic skills of the owner:** Examples include a classical pianist performing around the country, a stand-up comedian, or a theatre producer. Sure, you could team up with other artists in a similar field, but the actual core of what you do (such as playing virtuosic piano) is almost impossible to delegate.

>> **Businesses making products that require very specific skills, particularly those of an artistic nature:** For example, glass blowing, fine-art painting and pottery. Custom manufacturing of one-off goods also falls into this category, where the craftsperson (such as a cabinetmaker) builds a reputation that is very much linked to that person as an individual, rather than to the business.

>> **Businesses with expert services where the service provided is very much associated with the individual providing the service:** Think specialist medical professionals (acupuncturist, pediatrician, orthodontist) or specialist consultants (business mentors, human resources consultants).

>> **Businesses servicing a rural location where the owner provides the services and expansion involves too much travel:** Our local horse dentist (yes, such a thing as a horse dentist exists!) springs to mind.

If you have more of an entrepreneurial personality, you may be reading the preceding list thinking I'm lacking imagination, and that the businesses in the list could be expanded in plenty of ways. The artist could commercialize her images as cushions, postcards, or wallpaper; the cabinetmaker could spend oodles on high-end marketing and build up an international reputation; the horse dentist could set up an online consultancy. In my defense, I'm not saying that these businesses are impossible to grow — I'm just saying they're harder to grow than others. (And, besides, the artist may not want to design wallpaper, and online horse dentistry may prove massively impractical.)

TIP

If your business falls into one of the categories outlined in the preceding list and you're having problems imagining how you separate yourself from your business, hop online and search worldwide for the product you sell or the service you provide. Look for examples of others similar to you and how they have grown their business to be something bigger.

REMEMBER

Although businesses with expert services can be hard to expand, for those who manage to do so and build a network of professionals who provide a high consistency of service, the rewards can be substantial.

Chapter **5**

Exploiting Opportunities and Avoiding Threats

A *SWOT analysis* (SWOT stands for Strengths, Weaknesses, Opportunities and Threats) is a keystone for any business plan.

The idea is that you make a frank analysis of what your business is good at and what it's not. Next, you think about all the possible opportunities for your business, such as new markets, new products, or new ways of doing things. Last, you take a look at the threats facing your business, such as the state of the economy, industry trends, or fearsome competitors.

With this process complete, you play the divine game of matchmaker, looking to see if any business opportunities make a natural match for your strengths. Conversely, you look to see if any threats present an unhappy synergy with your weaknesses.

A SWOT analysis done in this way provides an ideal starting point for strategic planning, and is fundamental to business success. In this chapter, I explain how the whole deal works.

Rating Your Capabilities

I'm sure you don't have to pause for very long to think of someone who always seems to seek challenges in their life. Maybe you have a friend who's dyslexic but has chosen to be a linguist as a career, or you know someone in a wheelchair who loves to travel the world.

Chasing one's dreams and persisting in the face of adversity is often deeply rewarding. However, in the world of business, you will find that it usually pays to be more strategic about where you channel your energies. What you want to do is identify possible business opportunities, and see if you can match these opportunities against your natural skills and abilities.

Putting yourself through the griller

As part of objectively assessing your strengths and weaknesses, it's good to think about business skills, and assess both your own capabilities against each of these skills, as well as the importance of this skill to your business. Table 5-1 provides a simple checklist against which you can rate yourself and business importance on a scale of 1 to 5, with 5 being the highest rating.

TABLE 5-1 **Rating Your Capabilities**

Business Skill	How You Rate Yourself (1 to 5)	Importance to Your Business (1 to 5)
Ability to learn new skills and adapt quickly		
Bookkeeping and financial systems		
Branding, packaging and presentation		
Budgeting, cost analysis and reporting		
Business strategy		
Cashflow management		
Company management and compliance		

Business Skill	How You Rate Yourself (1 to 5)	Importance to Your Business (1 to 5)
Customer service culture		
IT and business systems		
Legal systems and protection		
Marketing and promotions		
Product design and development		
Professional expertise specific to your industry		
Sales and customer relations		
Social media and marketing		
Staff management		

REMEMBER

When you complete the ratings in Table 5-1, respond from the perspective of your business, rather than from you as an individual. Think of the collective skills that you, your employees, any family members, business mentors, or outside consultants bring to the party. Also, keep your competition in mind when you rate your business on things such as customer service or marketing. (For example, you may be aware of areas where you can improve your customer service but if you know that you beat all of your competition hands down, you can probably award yourself a pretty strong rating.)

WARNING

When rating how important each function is for your business, I suggest you rate all aspects of financial management as 4 or 5 (the highest rating). Even if your business chugs along just fine, poor financial management is almost always a limiter to business success and growth.

Prioritizing where you need to do better

If I'm a psychologist running a counselling business, chances are that cold calling or IT skills aren't going to be key to business success. On the other hand, if I'm selling a new product that few people have ever heard of, business strategy, branding and product design become essential.

Returning to Table 5-1, see if you can spot any business skills where you've rated yourself poorly, but where you've assessed the importance of this skill to your business as being high. These are areas of weaknesses in your business to which you need to pay attention, either by upskilling yourself or by employing staff, contractors, or advisers who can help fill the gap.

Identifying Opportunities and Threats

Industry trends aren't the only things that can greatly affect your business but over which you have little control. What about changes in the economy, or the arrival of new competitors on the scene? For you to stay one step ahead, the name of the game is to try to anticipate the impact these outside factors may have on your business.

For each of the following categories, ask yourself what opportunities and what threats lie in store. Remember that any change can be an opportunity or a threat (or even both) depending on where you stand in the scheme of things. Organize these opportunities and threats in two columns, similar to Table 5-2. (Although bear in mind that Table 5-2 is a somewhat simplified example — your list will almost certainly have a bit more detail.)

Consider the following:

>> **New competition:** How likely is it that new competitors could affect your business? Do you have special skills or a strategic advantage that safeguards you from competition? (I talk more about strategic advantage in Chapter 2.) Or is the thing that makes your business so successful easy to copy? What if the competitor has more capital, a better location, or superior marketing abilities?

TABLE 5-2 ## Summarizing Opportunities and Threats

Opportunities	Threats
Analysis for Elgin Craft Brewery	
New tourist trail being developed by local municipality — potential to join this	Growth in number of competitors
	Rising costs of supplies, energy, taxes and interest rates
Use of AI for swift product development	
	Takeovers of small breweries by large conglomerates, thereby devaluing the craft beer experience
Demand from customers seeking something different from mainstream suppliers	
	Cost of finance increasing
Opportunity to create short-term brands and product offerings responsive to trends and events	
Analysis for solar panel installation company	
Customers more discerning about types of panels and nature of installation	Some serious new competitors with major muscle
Government subsidies in certain regional locations for installs	Exclusive distribution license ends in two years
Demand for batteries as well as panels is growing rapidly	Rapid growth requires high borrowings and puts pressure on cashflow
	If new government elected, all subsidies could finish

>> **Emerging technologies:** How is technological change affecting your industry? Could new technology end up putting you out of business? Or are you skilled in the direction that new technology is heading, and could this be an opportunity?

>> **Changes in demographics:** Demographic change is a long-term thing, but so (hopefully) is your business. If your business serves a local population (as opposed to having national distribution or being online), it pays to watch the trends in population patterns for your area.

>> **Changes in government regulations:** If your business is dependent in some way on government regulations (maybe you're a taxi driver, you work in health, or your business relies heavily on government policy in some form or other),

you're particularly vulnerable to changes in the political landscape. Ask yourself what impact changing regulations or changes in government could have on your business, and how you could respond.

» **Changes in the economy:** Is your business very dependent on the ebb and flow of the economy? Some businesses (for example, those selling staple food products) are relatively stable regardless of what's happening in the economy; other businesses (such as those selling high-end luxury goods) tend to move in tandem with the economy.

When you're thinking about opportunities and threats for your business, you may also wish to do something called a *PESTEL analysis* (PESTEL stands for Political, Economic, Social, Technological, Environmental and Legal). This analysis, for which you'll easily find a template online, gets you to think more analytically about all outside factors that influence your business, such as the economy, the demographics of your target market, and the average profitability and trends of your industry.

The idea of analyzing the overall environment in this way is to identify the drivers of change affecting future industry growth. Of course, an industry that's in decline is going to be a whole load tougher (if not impossible) to succeed in than an industry that's growing very fast.

AN OPPORTUNITY OR A THREAT?

One overriding long-term global trend that's unlikely to change any time soon is the demand for ecological products and services. Couple this with global zero emission targets, and you end up with a perfect example of something that is both a business opportunity and a business threat.

For those in the 'green' industry (ecological products, renewable energy, environmental consulting and so on) this long-term trend presents an opportunity. For those in industries with high energy demands, particularly those dependent on fossil fuels, this trend is a threat.

TIP

Keep your mind open to the fact that some things don't fit neatly into boxes as an opportunity or as a threat. Be willing to get creative. Although your analysis of threats and opportunities usually reflects your current position, stay open to new possibilities.

Doing a SWOT Analysis

If you've read any other business books or worked in larger organizations, you've probably already heard of a SWOT analysis (Strengths, Weaknesses, Opportunities and Threats). As a model, the SWOT analysis sticks around while other business concepts come and go, simply because this way of looking at things is both easy to understand and surprisingly powerful.

Putting theory into practice

The idea of a SWOT analysis is simple:

>> Aim to build on your strengths but minimize your weaknesses.

>> Endeavor to seize opportunities and counteract threats.

Are you ready to try your own SWOT analysis? Then here goes:

1. **Make a list of the strengths and weaknesses of your business.**

   By strengths and weaknesses, I'm talking about the things that you and your staff are good at (or not-so-good at). I explain how to assess your strengths and weaknesses earlier in this chapter in 'Putting yourself through the griller'.

   When you think about strengths and weaknesses, this is an internal examination just of you and your business.

REMEMBER

2. **Make a list of possible opportunities and threats.**

   Identifying opportunities and threats is an external analysis that looks outwards beyond your business, to consider your industry, the economy, the environment and other factors. Refer to 'Identifying Opportunities and Threats' to find out how to make this list.

3. **Draw a grid similar to Figure 5-1.**

4. **Divide your strengths into two categories: Strengths that can help you take advantage of opportunities, and strengths that can help you deal with threats.**

5. **Write down these strengths in the first row of your SWOT grid, along with the related opportunities or threats.**

   Strengths that help realize opportunities go in the top-left of the grid; strengths that could help counteract threats go in the top-right.

6. **In the same manner, divide your weaknesses into two categories: weakness that may hinder you taking advantage of opportunities, and weaknesses that may make threats even more of a threat.**

7. **Write down these weaknesses, as well as the threats, in the second row of your SWOT grid.**

   Weaknesses that hinder opportunities go in the bottom-left of the grid; weaknesses that exacerbate threats go in the bottom-right.

Business SWOT Analysis		
	OPPORTUNITIES	**THREATS**
STRENGTHS	Write strengths that assist with opportunities here, along with a description of the opportunity	Write strengths that help counteract threats here, along with a description of the threat
WEAKNESSES	Write weaknesses that may hinder you from exploiting opportunities here, along with a description of the opportunity	Write weaknesses that may compound threats here, along with a description of the threat

FIGURE 5-1: The principles of a SWOT analysis.

Translating your SWOT analysis into action

After you've completed your SWOT analysis (refer to the preceding section), what next? Put simply, this grid encapsulates four different business strategies:

>> Aim to exploit any areas where your business is strong and is a good fit for an opportunity.

>> Keep a watchful eye on any areas where your business is strong, but a threat may be looming.

>> Try to improve on any areas where your business is weak but opportunities exist. (For example, you could consider

getting extra training, hiring employees with different skills, or employing consultants.)

>> Take pre-emptive action and attempt to get rid of any areas in which your business is weak and a threat is looming.

Figure 5-2 shows a SWOT grid in action, matching strengths and weaknesses of the craft brewing company used as an example earlier in this chapter with the identified opportunities and threats, as follows:

>> **Top-left corner (where a strength meets an opportunity):** Strong marketing skills are a good fit for growth in customer demand; the company can quickly leverage new brands. The business should aim to exploit these strengths.

>> **Top-right corner (where a strength meets a threat):** Strong marketing skills also serve to mitigate the threat of rapidly increasing competition. The business needs to keep a watchful eye on both its marketing strategy and new competitors.

>> **Bottom-left corner (where a weakness meets an opportunity):** A significant weakness is technological expertise, with a reliance on old methods of brewing rather than use of technology and AI to develop new flavors. The business should aim to develop skills swiftly, possibly by hiring employees with these skills.

>> **Bottom-right corner (where a weakness meets a threat):** The weaknesses in financial management may create problems in the face of rising costs and increased interest rates. This combination of weakness and threat create an unhappy synergy, indicating an area in which the business needs to take action.

Business SWOT Analysis		
	OPPORTUNITIES	THREATS
STRENGTHS	*Strong marketing skills are a good fit for growth in customer demand; company can quickly leverage new brands*	*Strong marketing skills will assist in meeting the challenges of many new competitors*
WEAKNESSES	*Weakness in technological expertise, with a reliance on old methods of brewing rather than use of technology and AI to develop new flavors*	*Weaknesses in financial management skills indicates vulnerability in the face of rising costs and increased interest rates*

FIGURE 5-2: Plotting business strategy using a SWOT analysis.

Creating a Plan for Change

In some ways, creating a business plan can be very 'bitty'. You have missions and visions and financials and marketing plans, then industry analysis and more. Each area feels like a separate topic in its own right, and may even require that you use a different mindset or different skills as you address each one. However, as you delve deeper and deeper into the process, you hopefully find that everything starts connecting.

At the beginning of this book, in Chapters 2 and 3, I talk about identifying your strategic advantage and analyzing how your business compares to the competition. In many ways, the industry analysis and SWOT analysis in this chapter follow a similar process, but provide another layer of clarity regarding what areas in your business to exploit, as well as the weaknesses to guard against.

In your business plan, try to include the following:

>> The issues or problems you face

>> The opportunities that lie ahead

>> A plan of action that outlines how you intend to mitigate your problems and exploit these opportunities

When drawing up a plan of action, try to express this plan in clear goals that are very specific and which have a time frame. For example, 'A weakness in our business is our financial management skills. We intend to hire an external accountant as a business advisor who we will meet with monthly'. Or another example: 'A clear weakness in my business is my poor marketing skills. As well as doing a small business course in the coming months, I intend to employ a contractor to manage my social media and PR campaigns'.

REMEMBER

Are you a person who sees the glass half-full or half-empty? Sure, threats may be on the horizon, but do opportunities lie within these threats? As Winston Churchill is widely (although incorrectly) attributed to have said, 'A pessimist sees the difficulty in every opportunity; an optimist sees the opportunity in every difficulty'.

IN THIS CHAPTER

» Structuring a marketing plan

» Crafting your point of difference and positioning statement

» Articulating who you want your customers to be

» Fine-tuning sales goals and objectives

» Developing a broad range of marketing strategies

» Pulling the pieces together

Chapter **6**

Developing a Smart Marketing Plan

By its very nature, marketing is a creative process, with the risk that marketing activities are driven more by impulse and instinct than by strategies and data. For this reason, I find creating a structured marketing plan is every bit as important as creating a detailed financial plan.

In this chapter, I talk about the elements that make up a marketing plan, and look at the important groundwork required to develop a distinctive brand and marketing strategy. What is it you're really selling and who do you want to sell this to? How do you set realistic sales targets and put strategies in place to make sure these targets are met? This chapter helps you answer such questions.

The format of your marketing plan depends on whether you're creating a standalone document or whether your marketing plan is part of a larger business plan document, and I talk about what information you might include in your plan at the end of this chapter.

Laying Down the Elements of Your Plan

Spend an hour or two browsing through different business resources and you're likely to find a dozen different formats for marketing plans. No right or wrong way exists to creating a plan, and indeed just articulating something in a structured fashion is 90 percent of the battle. Having said this, here are some of the elements of a marketing plan I suggest you include:

>> **Introduction:** An introduction provides background on who you are, what you're selling, the brand you're trying to build, any market research you've completed, and how you compare against competitors. (I talk about most of these topics in the following section.)

>> **Competitor analysis:** In this part of your marketing plan, you describe who your competitors are, and how you compare to them. Chapter 3 focuses on competitor analysis, but in this chapter (also in the following section) I talk about condensing this information and developing a positioning statement.

>> **Target market:** Who are your customers, and what are the demographics and psychographics of the customers you most want to reach? Later in this chapter, 'Defining Your Target Market' explains how to develop descriptions of your customers, and what channels you might use to reach them.

>> **Sales targets:** How much are you going to sell, who are you going to sell to, and what is your pricing strategy? See 'Setting Sales Targets', later in this chapter, for details.

>> **Marketing strategies:** What marketing strategies do you intend to put in place? Later in this chapter, 'Deciding on Your Marketing Strategies' outlines possible tactics, the importance of developing a marketing budget, and the importance of planning for customer service.

>> **Connecting the different elements:** The last section of this chapter, 'Connecting the Dots', explains how to bring all these different elements together to create a coherent marketing plan.

Selling the Hole (and Not the Drill)

In Chapter 2, I suggest that you start your business plan with a strategic advantage statement that explains how your product or service benefits your customers, and what differentiates your business from its competitors. As I explain in Chapter 2, this strategic advantage could be many things, including having lower costs, a brilliant new idea, specialist skills, or a right to use certain intellectual property.

Your marketing plan needs to do the following:

>> Reiterate this strategic advantage.

>> Consider how this advantage gives you an edge on competitors.

>> Express this edge succinctly in a way that interests and attracts customers.

When you're selling this difference to customers, your aim is to encapsulate this message in just a few words. This becomes what is known as your *USP* — your unique selling proposition.

TIP

If you're struggling to express your unique selling proposition, go online and search for businesses similar to your own. For example, maybe you offer a piano-tuning service. Search for similar businesses all around the world and check out their marketing slogans: 'Technicians with 20 years' experience', 'Advanced technology for unbeatable accuracy', 'Event and concert specialists'. I'm not suggesting you pinch someone else's selling proposition; rather, you can lean on these ideas for inspiration.

In Table 6-1, I list some examples and demonstrate how a unique selling proposition is both clearly related to, but very different from, a strategic advantage.

TIP

The beauty of developing your own USP is that you can hone in on the thing that makes you different from your competitors, which is an infinitely better approach than trying to be all things to all people. Have a think about what you want your USP to be (or what it already is) and how you can best exploit this in your overall marketing.

TABLE 6-1 **Strategic Advantage versus Unique Selling Proposition**

Type of Business	Strategic Advantage	USP
Bookseller	Owner was formerly a respected publisher and is super well connected with authors around the country	'Exclusive access to author interviews and signed editions'
Carpenter	Specialist training in CAD software as well as a partner trained in interior design	'Help us to visualize and construct the interiors of your dreams'
Copywriting service	Strong working relationship with offshore subcontractor in different time zone	'24-hour service and swift turnarounds'
Games developer	Educational specialist with unique game mechanics	'Specializing in game development for middle grade'
Musician	Phenomenal ability to memorize songs and lyrics	'Live performances of playlists of your choice'
Naturopath	Qualifications in both counselling and naturopathy	'A holistic service for body and mind'
Your business... (fill in the blanks)	*Your strategic advantage...* (fill in the blanks)	*Your USP...* (fill in the blanks)

The final piece of the puzzle for the introduction of the marketing plan is to create a *competitor positioning statement*, a succinct description of how you want your brand to be perceived when compared to that of your competitors. This statement usually follows the format 'Target audience . . . category/market . . . key differentiator . . . primary competitor . . . point of difference'. (You may need to scoot back to Chapter 3 for how to perform a competitive analysis and confirm your competitive strategy.)

So, for example, if you're starting an eco-tourism guiding business, your statement might be something like, 'For environmentally conscious adventurers, Eco Guides offers small-sized sustainable and ethical tours with a focus on connecting with nature. We differ from traditional tour operators, which although they may have low prices, often have large group sizes and a significant carbon footprint'.

Your marketing plan must articulate what it is that you do better or differently than your competitors, and position your business against these competitors in a way that it is clear you can succeed.

Defining Your Target Market

Key to any marketing plan is a description of your target market. For established businesses, defining your target market is largely about analyzing who your current customers are; for businesses just getting started, defining your target market is about describing who you hope your customers are going to be.

Sometimes you may find that your customers end up being a different kind of customer than what you originally anticipated. You may be fine with this, or you may decide that you want to change your mix of customers. In this situation, you need to implement specific sales targets and strategies to effect this change.

Playing with customer persona

The more niche and specific your marketing tactics, the more likely you are to succeed. One excellent way to ensure your marketing is targeted in the right way is to create three to five different customer persona — by *persona*, I mean archetypal representations of existing or target customers.

For example, imagine I'm trying to market a writers festival in a regional town. I know from previous years the kind of audience members who buy tickets, and I have a sense of how I might group them. My next step is to organize my thinking into archetypes of three ideal customers.

My first customer persona is Alex, a 67-year-old retired social worker who lives nearby, loves to read books, is well off and is highly politically aware. My second persona is Emma, a 40-year-old aspiring writer who works as an editor but is keen to publish her memoir. Emma lives two hours' drive away, but likes to go for weekends away with her friends. Then I have Ishara, a working parent with three kids. Ishara lives nearby, is always looking for things for her kids to do on weekends, and is interested in parenting, neurodiversity, and the environment.

I then make up little stories about each customer, describing their education, values, and relationships, and maybe adding photos and other personal touches. I consider aspects such as age, gender, interests, and lifestyle, as well as the challenges or problems this person is facing.

Next, I think about the marketing strategies for each persona. Alex lives locally, and I decide to reach him via posters, ads in the local paper, and postcards at the bookshop. Emma is trickier, but my marketing strategies include personalized emails, targeted Facebook and Instagram posts, and targeted ads on book-related sites. With Ishara, articles in parenting blogs, posters at the preschools and Instagram posts are my strategies.

The number of personas you should have depends on the size of your business, but three to five personas is ample to begin with. Remember that the idea is to create a tailored marketing strategy for each persona, and so the work required escalates with each persona you add.

TIP

If you're analyzing your existing customer base, keep in mind that each persona represents not just an existing market segment, but rather an ideal market segment. Don't spend time developing personas built on the kind of customers who are more trouble than they are worth. The idea of visualizing personas is to spend time thinking about what your ideal customer looks like, and then target marketing resources to reach that group.

Thinking creatively about channels

In the next part of your marketing plan, devote some space to *channel analysis*. Sounds technical, but channel analysis is simply a description of each channel that you plan to sell through. Here are a few examples of channel analysis:

>> Nina has a retail store in the suburbs. However, she also sells some clothes online. Her shop is one channel; online sales are another.

>> A manufacturer making gourmet jams sells through three different channels: Direct to stores, in bulk to distributors, and direct to consumers at farmers' markets.

>> Anita makes jewelry. She sells some at the markets herself, some to a local gift store, and some through a party plan. Each of these outlets is a channel.

>> An importer sells furniture via four different channels: Large department stores, independent stores, online via a distributor's website, and direct to customers from the warehouse shopfront.

Do you sell to more than one channel? (And, if not, maybe you should!) Then devote some of your marketing plan to describing each channel. Analyze what proportion of your sales goes to each channel, and whether this channel is growing or declining.

Setting Sales Targets

Setting sales targets can be challenging even if you've been trading for many years, but is particularly difficult if you're starting a new venture. Nevertheless, a marketing plan without sales targets is no kind of plan at all.

Here are my three hot tips for setting sales targets that work:

>> **Slice goals into bite-sized chunks.** Avoid plucking random figures out of the air. Instead, break sales target into bite-sized chunks, setting targets as to the number of units sold per week, the number of regions reached, or the number of tickets sold for each event.

>> **Set goals that are about more than just money.** For example, you might set a goal to create a business that's more inclusive and welcoming, a goal to expand into a specific suburb, a goal to increase repeat business, or a goal to improve booking rates (conversions) from email queries.

>> **Get SMART with your goals.** Ensure your goals are Specific, Measurable, Achievable, Realistic and Time-bound. Can you measure every goal in terms of units sold or customers gained? Are your goals both achievable and realistic? And have you set a time frame for each goal?

Deciding on Your Marketing Strategies

When it comes to marketing strategies, many people get stuck in their comfort zone. After all, few people enjoy cold calling, business networking meetings can be very hard on the introverts among us, and most PR activities require a high level of communication skills.

Only you can decide what marketing strategies are best for your business, but in this next part of the chapter, I encourage you to explore strategies you may not have considered. In this way, you're way more likely to end up with a marketing plan that is both well rounded and effective.

Brainstorming different strategies

Consider how you might apply each one of the following marketing strategies to your business:

>> **Advertising:** Traditional print media, online advertising such as Facebook or Google Ads, and radio advertising.

>> **Community engagement:** Partnering with other local businesses, hosting events, volunteering, and sponsoring community programs.

>> **Content marketing:** Advice, information or news that could be interesting to your customers delivered via blogs, newsletters, social media, podcasts, video channels, and your website.

>> **In-store promotions:** Seasonal sales, bundle deals, point systems, birthday rewards, samples, free trials, contests, giveaways, limited-time offers, and events.

>> **Loyalty programs:** Reward cards, membership benefits, special pricing, exclusive content, and point systems.

>> **Partnerships and networking:** Collaborations, cross-promotions, sponsorships, and networking functions.

>> **Public relations:** Press releases, media kits, and feature articles.

>> **Social media:** Facebook, Instagram, TikTok, YouTube, and X.

TIP

If you're struggling to think of how to apply any one of the preceding strategies to your business, try using an AI tool such as ChatGPT. Use the question 'How could I use a marketing strategy of [insert strategy here] for my [insert type of business here]?' to generate some fresh ideas you may not have considered up until now. For example, 'How could I use a loyalty program for my bookstore business?'

Choosing a marketing strategy mix

Steering clear of personal preferences and prioritizing sales strategies objectively can be very tricky. With this in mind, here's my suggested plan of action:

1. **Read through the list of marketing strategies in this chapter.**

    Refer to the section 'Brainstorming different strategies'.

2. **Get together with your business partners, staff, colleagues, or advisers, and arrange a marketing meeting.**

    If the business is just you, find somebody you trust to bounce ideas off.

3. **Brainstorm different marketing ideas.**

    Remember the rules of brainstorming — even if someone comes up with an idea that's hopeless, or something that seems ridiculous pops into your head, you can't judge. Simply write down the idea and keep going.

4. **When the brainstorming process starts winding down, stop generating new ideas and instead highlight the 15 or so best ideas.**

REMEMBER

    Ensure you have ideas that relate to at least three of the marketing strategies listed in the section 'Brainstorming different strategies'. For example, don't restrict your marketing to social media or to advertising, but go beyond your comfort zone to include other strategies such as content marketing or community engagement.

5. **Next to the 15 best ideas, write approximate costs and the amount of time required. Score through any ideas that are plainly unaffordable or unachievable.**

    Don't forget to think about your target market at this point (refer to 'Defining Your Target Market', earlier in this chapter).

You may need to generate different marketing strategies for the different kinds of customers you want to reach.

6. **Rank these ideas in order of most impact.**

   Don't worry about how much these ideas cost or how long they may take at this point.

7. **Select the combination of ideas that you feel will give you most bang for your buck and cross out any ideas that you know will be unaffordable.**

   Make sure you continue to have a combination of ideas across the range of strategies listed in 'Brainstorming different strategies'.

8. **With the amount of time you have available in mind, number your remaining ideas, starting with the number 1.**

   So idea 'number 1' will be within your marketing budget, achievable in a reasonable amount of time, and guaranteed or very likely to generate sales. (If you still have more than 10 ideas on your list at this point, score through any ideas numbered 11 or higher.)

You now have a list of marketing strategies, numbered in order of priority. The next step is to cost these strategies and determine whether you can afford them. Read on. . .

Developing a marketing budget

Once you've set your sales targets (refer to 'Setting Sales Targets', earlier in this chapter) and created a list of possible marketing strategies (refer to the preceding section), the next step is to figure out how much these strategies will cost to deliver, and whether this is affordable.

WARNING

Determining the right amount for your marketing budget is tricky, not least if you're at a start-up phase and your budget is tight. Even if finances are tight, however, try to avoid the pitfall of spending too little on marketing, especially in the early stages of building a business. In the ideal world, research what percentage of revenue other businesses similar to your own are spending on marketing, and try to allocate this amount at least. (For small businesses, this is often between 5 and 10 percent of revenue, but you will probably need to allocate additional funds in the first couple of years of trading, particularly if you want to build brand awareness.)

Your marketing budget should list all planned marketing activities and their associated expenses, and include a timeline that spreads your budget across the year ahead. Start by costing each one of your proposed marketing strategies and then assess what you can realistically achieve. It may be that you need to focus on one target market at a time, or that you spread your activities over a year or more, testing each strategy as you go to evaluate its return on investment.

If you're spending money on online advertising, particularly if you have an e-commerce business, endeavor to set up some form of conversion tracking so that you track the cost of acquiring a customer or making a sale. For example, if you spend $500 on Facebook advertising and this leads to the acquisition of 20 new customers, that's $25 per customer. Calculating conversion costs in this way is a great way of trialing different marketing channels and comparing their performance.

Keeping customers front of mind

Ask successful businesspeople what they think their secret is, and chances are they say something about their customers. In fact, the majority of established businesses list customer service right at the top of attributes vital to their success.

Doing the right thing by your customers is the best possible form of marketing. The way you treat your customers influences their decision to come back to you. Customers are also getting more and more vocal about the value they place on being treated properly, so listening to your customers reaps rewards. If something matters to your customers, it has to matter to you, too.

Customer service does mean different things to different people. I've heard excellent service described as 'being at your best with every customer' or 'figuring out new ways to help people'. Regardless of the description, the principle remains the same for all businesses — excellent service means always doing the right things, in the ways customers want them done. Applying this principle in practice depends entirely on your business.

As part of your marketing plan, I suggest you include a few paragraphs summarizing your customer service plan. In particular, you may want to include:

>> Customer service goals (for example, your target response time for enquiries or order turnaround time)

>> How you plan to seek feedback from customers

>> How your customer service standards compare with the competition

>> How you intend to guarantee the consistency and quality of your products and/or services

Similar to your sales targets, your customer service goals should ideally be SMART (Specific, Measurable, Achievable, Realistic and Time-bound).

Connecting the Dots

Pulling together the many strands of a marketing plan is tricky, not least because of the whole chicken-and-egg nature of the beast. For example, you may start by defining your target market but then, once you progress to considering your preferred marketing strategies, this changes the way you're thinking about your target market.

However, here's a summary of what I've covered in this chapter, as well as how to link the different elements together:

1. **Articulate your unique selling proposition.**

   Refer to 'Selling the Hole (and Not the Drill)', earlier in this chapter.

2. **Describe how you will position yourself against competitors.**

   Refer to 'Selling the Hole (and Not the Drill)', earlier in this chapter.

3. **Define your target market, possibly using a handful of customer persona to bring clarity.**

   Refer to 'Defining Your Target Market', earlier in this chapter. The level of detail you provide here may depend on whether you're writing a standalone marketing plan, or whether your marketing plan forms part of an overall business plan.

4. **Set sales targets for the year ahead, providing as much detail as possible.**

I talk about this in 'Setting Sales Targets', earlier in this chapter. Of course, if your business plan spans a longer period than the next 12 months, these sales targets will need to span a longer period also.

5. **Brainstorm different marketing strategies, keeping an open mind about all the possibilities.**

Your final marketing plan or business plan will simply articulate the strategies you land on, but at this stage it pays to consider as many possibilities as you can.

6. **With target markets, customer persona and marketing strategies in mind, itemize how much you intend to spend on each marketing activity.**

At this point, you may find you need a few iterations of your plan. With the budget you have available, can you afford to deliver on the marketing strategies you've selected? Do you have sufficient funds to reach all of your desired target markets? With this in mind, are your sales targets possible?

In your final marketing plan or business plan, a simple summary of intended marketing expenditure is probably sufficient.

7. **Settle on a timeline for the next 12 months at least that lists marketing activities and how much each one will cost to deliver.**

Ideally, this list of activities relates strongly to your favored marketing strategies, your desired target markets and, of course, your budget. Again, the level of detail you include here depends on whether this is a standalone marketing plan or part of a bigger document.

8. **Describe how you're going to review and evaluate your marketing plan.**

Although sometimes more of an art than a science, the calculation of return on investment (ROI) of each marketing activity is crucial. Google Analytics, conversion tracking, budgets versus actual reporting, and referral source reporting are all examples of ways you can track the effectiveness of your marketing initiatives.

IN THIS CHAPTER

» **Making a list of everything you need, and how much it's likely to cost**

» **Differentiating between start-up expenses and ongoing business expenses**

» **Calculating how much finance your business requires to get off the ground**

» **Taking out loans, looking for investors and more**

Chapter **7**
Budgeting for Start-Up Expenses

I f you're planning to start a new business or expand your existing business in some way, chances are you're going to need a bit of capital behind you. The question is, of course, how much?

When starting a business, you need to budget not only for capital items such as new equipment, vehicles, and merchandise, but also for the variety of additional expenses you're bound to encounter in the first few months of trading. You may also need additional finance for living expenses until your business becomes profitable. This detail is essential to the budget you include in your business plan, and calculating how much finance, if any, you need to secure.

In this chapter, I talk about how to calculate how much start-up capital you're going to need. I also talk about the pros and cons of business loans, credit cards, equity partners, outside investors, leases, and last (but not least) borrowing funds from benevolent friends and family.

Creating a Start-Up Budget

Creating a budget for start-up expenses is a good idea, no matter how large or small your proposed business. Unless you know how much capital you're going to need to get started, you won't have any idea about how much finance is required, nor will you have a sense of the risk involved.

TIP

If you're still at the conception stage for your business — maybe you're testing your product at local markets or trialing the service that you offer — you're probably still working from home or manufacturing on a small scale. As part of the planning process and testing the long-term viability of your business idea, I suggest you create a start-up budget for how much money you would require if you were to manufacture your product on a large scale, or if you were to set up a proper office servicing a wide range of clients.

Estimating your start-up expenses

In Table 7-1, I show a possible format for a start-up budget. I suggest you create this list using a spreadsheet option such as Excel or Google Sheets or, if you're using business planning software, look to see if you can find a suitable template. (This way, if you change your forecasted figures, all the totals recalculate automatically.)

TABLE 7-1 **Start-up Expenses Budget**

Description of Start-up Expense	$
New Equipment or Tools	
Computers systems and accessories	
Motor vehicles, including special fit-out, if required	
Office furnishings	
Retail equipment (scanners, point-of-sale software)	
Tools and equipment	
Other (describe here) _____	

Description of Start-up Expense	$
Premises Fit-out	
Local government fees, if necessary	
Fit-out of new premises	
Lease agreement fees	
Rental bond and rent in advance	
Other (describe here) _____	
Other Start-up Expenses	
Accounting fees (advice for new start-up)	
Branding and logo design	
Consultant fees	
Contingency reserve (approx. 10 percent of start-up expenses)	
Incorporation of company	
Insurance (public liability/business indemnity/property insurance)	
IT infrastructure (servers, networks, cloud storage)	
Legal fees (incorporation, trademarks)	
License fees and permits	
Marketing launch expenses (including online advertising)	
Product development or content production	
Professional membership fees	
Registration of business name and domain name(s)	
Security bonds for electricity, gas, and telecommunications	
Signage	
Stock for resale	
Training and recruitment of staff	
Website design	
Other (describe here) _____	
TOTAL	$__.__

Here are some pointers to help along the way:

» The start-up expenses listed in Table 7-1 are generic, and you may well wish to add additional types of expenses specific to your business.

» Before adding items not listed in Table 7-1, remember that you're only budgeting for start-up expenses here, not operating expenses. (If you're not sure what counts as a start-up expense, skip ahead to the section 'Separating Start-up Expenses', later in this chapter.)

» Have you already paid for some start-up expenses using your own funds? See the following section for more details regarding whether to include these transactions in your start-up budget.

REMEMBER

» If consumer tax applies in the country or state in which you're operating (for example, sales tax in the United States, VAT in Canada or the United Kingdom, or GST in Australia and New Zealand), and you know that you will be able to claim a refund for any tax you pay, show your start-up expenses excluding, rather than including, tax.

REMEMBER

I'm often asked how much is reasonable for a start-up budget. My answer is that I've seen business start-ups that require not one brass razoo, and others that require several million dollars. If you're not sure about the accuracy (or completeness) of your start-up budget, I suggest you bounce the figures off your accountant, business adviser, or a colleague working in the industry.

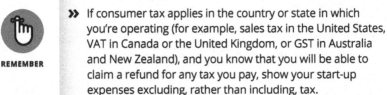
TIP

One thing I have noticed is that people planning a new retail business often seem to underestimate start-up expenses. Items such as shop fit-out and opening stock are invariably more expensive than expected. Make sure you're budgeting enough to cover all likely expenses.

Including expenses paid for out of personal funds

Have you already purchased an asset in your own name that you're intending to use for business purposes (likely examples are a computer or vehicle)? If so, should you show this item in your budget for start-up expenses? The answer depends, as follows:

>> If you're setting up as a sole trader or a partnership, your start-up budget doesn't need to include assets that you've already purchased (although at tax time, do remember to let your accountant know).

>> If your business is going to have a company structure and you require the company to reimburse you straightaway for this asset, then, yes, include this asset in your start-up budget.

>> If your business is going to have a company structure but you're happy for the company to make use of an asset that you own while it's getting established, you don't need to include this asset in your start-up budget. Talk to your accountant, because they may recommend that you show this item as a company asset, and the debt to you as a company liability.

Adding enough to live on

Most businesses don't make any profit in the first six months and, in fact, many businesses make a loss during this time. For some businesses, the period before you see any profits may be even longer.

When budgeting for a new business, you not only need to budget for business expenses, but your own living expenses also. Quite how you do this depends on your circumstances, and whether you're continuing to work another job while your business gets established.

TIP

While your budget for start-up expenses is an essential first step, this budget doesn't necessarily provide a clear indication of how much you need as start-up capital— you only know that for sure when you complete the rest of your financial projections. See Chapter 11 for more details.

Separating Start-Up Expenses

If you're new to business, you may find it hard to differentiate between start-up expenses and operating expenses. This difference is crucial in order to calculate how much start-up finance is required and to report business profitability accurately.

A *start-up expense* is a one-off expense related to starting your business or purchasing an asset that your business requires. An *operating expense* is an ongoing expense that will feature as a regular part of running your business.

In terms of your business plan and financial reporting, but not necessarily your tax return, if something's a one-off expense that's related to getting your business started and you don't expect to have this expense again as part of day-to-day trading (or not for a little while at least), you should treat this as a start-up expense.

For example, if you rent a new office or shop and you spend money on fitting out the premises, building shelves, adding carpet or painting, these are good examples of start-up expenses. However, if you repaint or re-carpet the office in a few years' time, this would count as repairs and maintenance.

Other items such as logo design, branding, marketing materials, or packaging design are also good examples of start-up expenses. Sure, you'll almost certainly spend money on more marketing materials in the future, but you're unlikely to have such a big expense all in one go.

What you're trying to do is identify all those initial expenses that come in a rush when you first start up your business, and separate these from the ongoing expenses you're going to have with your business. This is the only way you can establish how profitable your business really is in those first financially delicate months of trading.

If you're a manufacturer, retailer, or wholesaler, your start-up budget also includes the initial purchase of products for resale.

Figuring Out How Much is Enough

Once you have a solid idea of how much start-up capital you require to get your business started, including funds to tide you over if your business takes a while to trade profitably, you can start thinking about three things:

>> If you don't have the necessary savings, will you be able to borrow the money? (See the following section for more information.)

>> How much will you need to borrow, and what will the likely repayments be?

>> If you need to take out a loan, will repayments be affordable in the first year or two of your business — or will this level of borrowing bring an unacceptable level of risk and/or stress?

Depending on the answers to these questions, you may want to review your start-up budget. Although earlier in this chapter I stress the importance of giving your business every possible chance of success by budgeting enough (refer to the section 'Creating a Start-up Budget'), you may find that you can pull back on or delay some spending without the business suffering unduly.

Here are some tips for pruning your start-up budget:

>> **Consider leasing rather than buying assets outright.** Finance that's secured against an asset such as a vehicle is usually pretty easy to obtain and preserves your working capital.

>> **Be realistic.** Although you may really want that new vehicle or piece of equipment, it may be more prudent to delay such purchases, or hire equipment and tools as needed.

>> **Consider buying stuff second-hand.** Buying second-hand might not be as glamorous, but may do the job just as well.

TIP

Always guard your working capital (that is, the difference between your current assets and current liabilities) as a tigress guards her cubs. You may indeed have enough in the bank to purchase everything your business needs to get started. However, if your business is successful and grows at any kind of pace at all, the growth itself may put strain on your cashflow.

Securing the Funds You Need

After deciding how much finance (if any) you require, the next task is to decide how best to secure this finance. In this section, I talk about different kinds of finance, and the pros and cons of each. (In Chapter 12, I take this a step further, and talk about how best to pitch for the finance you require as part of your business plan, and how you may want to present information differently when seeking a loan from a bank versus seeking funds from an investor.)

Banks are often the easiest option, but one of the decisions you need to make is what kind of bank finance is right for you. Business loans operate very differently from credit cards, as do leases or overdrafts.

However, you may find that no bank is willing to offer you finance, especially if you have no steady income and no collateral (that is, assets such as your home against which the bank secures its loan). Other sources of funds include outside investors, equity partners, or borrowing from family or friends.

This section touches on all of these sources of finance, but I do suggest you seek external advice before proceeding with any of these options.

Getting a bank loan (if you can)

Before you jump into a long-term relationship with any lender, be clear what you're getting into. Here's a quick summary of the kinds of finance typically offered by banking institutions:

>> A *business loan* usually works like an ordinary home loan — you borrow a fixed amount and commit to regular repayments over a certain number of years. A business loan is well suited for start-up finance, debt refinancing, or financing business growth.

REMEMBER

With business loans, the upside of structured repayments is that you're likely to pay off the loan relatively quickly. The downside is the bank usually offers a relatively short term on business loans (five years is quite standard), meaning that repayments are high in the early years when the business can least afford it.

>> A *business lease* can work in different ways depending on how you structure the lease. This kind of finance is almost always secured against a specific item of equipment or vehicle. Essentially, the finance company buys the asset on your behalf and then you make regular monthly payments

for an agreed amount of time. Depending on the lease agreement, you will either own the asset outright at the end of the loan term, or you will be able to purchase it for a reduced price.

TIP

Leases are relatively easy to obtain for existing businesses (because they're secured against the asset itself) and help preserve your valuable working capital for things that are harder to obtain finance for (such as an increase in inventory or financing of accounts receivable).

>> A *credit card* is the easiest type of finance to obtain, but is usually limited in how much you can borrow and involves the highest rate of interest. Generally, credit cards are best for short-term borrowing of relatively small amounts, and are a poor choice for start-up business finance.

>> A *microloan* is a small short-term small business loan, often provided by a non-profit organization or community bank that also offers support services for those just starting out.

>> A *line of credit* or *overdraft* works a little like a regular bank account, except the balance is in the red, not the black. You can use the loan for all your business banking, including both deposits and withdrawals. You have a credit limit on the account, and it's your choice whether you pay off the principal or pay interest only. Lines of credit are ideal for on-demand working capital and improved cashflow.

WARNING

Although a line of credit offers great flexibility for your business, you do need to have a disciplined nature to force yourself to pay off the debt. (If you never reduce the principal outstanding on your line of credit, you end up paying more interest than on a regular business loan.)

Offering up collateral

Almost all banks require some security against borrowings and, unless you're still renting, the most obvious security is usually your own home. While you probably feel reluctant to offer your home as security, you may find that you don't have much choice in the matter, or that a business loan secured against your home attracts substantially less interest than a business loan that's unsecured.

CROWD AROUND

Crowdfunding (also sometimes called crowdsourcing, crowd financing, or crowd fundraising) can be a solid way to raise funds for your business idea.

With *equity crowdfunding*, backers receive equity or shares in the company in return for their investment; with *reward-based crowdfunding*, backers receive a product or service; with *debt crowdfunding*, backers receive interest payments.

Are you wondering whether crowdfunding is a possible way that you could raise funds for your business? New crowdfunding platforms launch almost every day, but GoFundMe, Indiegogo, Kickstarter, LendingClub, Pozible and SeedInvest are all platforms with solid reputations and high participation rates.

Even if a business loan is in your name only, if you guarantee this loan against a property that's jointly owned, it's extremely likely that both parties (that is, both you and your best beloved) are jointly liable. This means that if the relationship breaks down, you get sick or even if you die, the other person may be legally obliged to repay the debt. For this reason, involving your better half in the decision about using the family home to secure a business loan is vital.

Seeking an outside investor

In the preceding sections, I talk only about *debt finance*, meaning that to get start-up capital for your business, you go into debt. However, the other major source of business finance is *equity finance*. With equity finance, you receive funding from an investor in exchange for a portion of ownership of your business.

The idea with most equity finance is that investors buy into your company, offering funds and expertise in return for part-ownership. The investors may receive low interest or minimal interest on these funds, with their goal being long-term capital gain. However, because such investors are exposed to the risk of your company failing, they usually look for businesses with a strong history of growth and higher-than-average returns.

The advantages of equity finance include the ability to raise funds even if you don't have security or collateral to offer, meaning that your financial structure is more stable. In addition, your business can hopefully benefit from the investor's management expertise. On the downside, an outside investor means that you no longer have complete control of your business. You may find not being able to make decisions without consulting others first hard, especially if you're used to running your own show, and conflict between you and the investor becomes a real possibility.

Note that for the purposes of writing a business plan, an outside investor is going to be interested in how they can get an above-average rate of return from your business. Outlining this for a potential investor likely means returning to that question of what it is about your business model that's so special. Skip ahead to Chapter 12 for more about framing your business plan for the eyes of investors.

Borrowing from family and friends

Borrowing from family or friends can be both the easiest and the hardest way to secure finance, all at the same time.

TRUE STORY

When first writing this chapter, I drafted the next couple of paragraphs about borrowing from family and friends and then decided, 'Nah, I'll just delete this stuff — it's all so obvious'. And so I did. The very next day, I bumped into the sister of an old client of mine and we got chatting. The father of my client had lent my client a large sum of money many years ago, and my client had repaid his father assiduously in the intervening period until the debt was completely cleared. As far as I was concerned, this particular scenario was a happy one, where none of the stuff that so often goes awry with family loans had occurred. Little did I know, the sister of my client, many years after this loan had been offered and then repaid, was still upset. It turned out that she had approached her father for finance as well, but her father had said he couldn't, because he had no money left to lend. The sister had missed out on the purchase of the farm she wanted, and had nursed resentment against her brother for years.

WARNING

You will find many ways to make money in your lifetime, but you will only have one family, and your family relationships are probably more valuable than anything else you have in your life. (I'm including here the friends in your life that may be your substitute family.) If you're considering borrowing from friends or family, pause first to think how this could affect your friendships or how your siblings may feel. If these relationships would suffer if you fail to repay these funds (and failure in business, no matter how optimistic you currently feel, is always possible), then think again. You may be better to borrow from a different source.

Chapter **8**

Figuring Out Prices and Predicting Sales

I f you're like most people starting out in business, you may be tempted to undercharge for your products or services. Maybe you're unsure about how much customers are willing to pay, or you're anxious that customers won't value your services. Maybe you're worried that you won't secure enough business to cover your expenses.

By undercharging, I'm talking about charging less than your customers are willing to pay. Precisely what this amount is can be tricky to judge, especially if you're pricing a service rather than a product. Calculating the value of your skills and expertise through the eyes of a customer is a very subjective process.

In this chapter, I talk about pricing strategies and how best to go about setting a price for your products or services. I also explain how to create your sales forecast for the next 12 months, one of the fundamental building blocks for any business plan.

Choosing a Pricing Strategy

Business educators use a heap of different terminology for price strategies, but essentially any price strategy boils down to one of three things: cost-based pricing, competitor-based pricing or value-based pricing. In the following sections I explore each strategy in turn.

Setting prices based on costs

Cost-based pricing is where you start by figuring out what it costs you to make a product or provide a service, and then you add an additional amount to arrive at the profit that you're after.

For example, imagine I decide to start a business selling sunhats at the local markets. The hats cost $8 each to buy, the stall costs $100 rent for the day and I reckon I can sell 50 hats a day. I want to make $250 profit to cover my time, so this means I decide to charge $15 per hat. (Sales of $15 × $50 = $750; less the $400 for the cost of the hats, less the rent of $100, and I'm left with $250 in my hot, sticky hand.)

This pricing model may sound like good business practice, but it's not, because this way of working doesn't pause to consider how much customers are actually prepared to pay for these hats. Maybe another stall opposite is selling the self-same hats for only $12. Maybe the hats are a real bargain and I should be charging $20.

WARNING

From a strategic perspective, cost-based pricing is the weakest of all business models. On the one hand, if the resulting prices are too high in relation to the competition, the business will flounder; on the other hand, if resulting prices are less than people are prepared to pay, you'll miss out on the possibility of above-average profits.

Setting prices based on competitors

Competitor-based pricing is where you look at what your competitors are charging for similar products or services, and then set your prices accordingly. This pricing strategy is the most common strategy used by business.

As I mention in the introduction to this chapter, if you're just starting out in business, you may fall foul of the temptation to be cheaper than everyone else. However, unless everyone else in the industry is driving around in sports cars with money to burn, chances are your competitors' prices are the level they are for a very good reason. Unless you have a strategic advantage that enables you to produce products or provide your services cheaper than your competitors (refer to Chapter 2), setting your prices lower than everyone else is likely to lead to poor profitability for you, as well as a risky business model.

Instead of trying to undercut competitors, look at the prices that your competitors are charging and use this analysis as a reflection of what the market is prepared to pay. Then pitch your pricing accordingly.

TIP

Competing on price alone is always a dangerous strategy. Sure, you need to be aware of competitor pricing and factor this information into your pricing decisions. However, how you position and sell your products and services should almost always be based on a combination of many different factors, such as quality of product or quality of service, delivery times, location, availability and ambience, and never just price alone. (For more about identifying your competitive strategy, refer to Chapter 3.)

Setting prices based on perceived value

Value-based pricing is where you reflect on the products or services you provide, look at the customer demand, and then set your price according to how much you think customers will be prepared to pay.

Here are a few examples of value-based pricing:

>> Apple use value-based pricing for many of their products (sought-after items such as iPads and iPhones), where no direct head-to-head competition exists and customers are prepared to pay premium prices for a brand on which they place a high value.

>> The stallholders selling umbrellas outside the city train station close to where I live push up the price of umbrellas by $3 or $4 every time it rains. Why? Because customers place a much higher value on staying dry when the rain is bucketing down.

In many ways, value-based pricing represents the essence of good business sense and marketing. After all, how better to set your prices than by judging the maximum that customers are willing to pay? The only tricky thing about value-based pricing is that any judgment is subjective. For example, I love the design of Apple's gear and will happily pay premium dollars for a new iPhone. My son Daniel, however, doesn't place much value on Apple's design and prefers generic products. Therefore, the value Daniel places on an iPhone is significantly less than the value I place on the same item.

Building a Hybrid-Pricing Plan

So far in this chapter, I've been talking about the theory of pricing and different pricing strategies. However, most successful businesses don't employ a single price strategy but instead employ a combination of strategies.

An example is a luxury inner-city hotel. Most of the time, the owners use competitive-based pricing, setting rates with the awareness of competitors' pricing very much in mind. However, with their premium rooms, they use value-based pricing, often improvising rates on the spot according to demand and what they think customers will be prepared to pay. Finally, for last-minute rates where they have a bunch of empty rooms and they know they won't be able to fill all of them, they use cost-based pricing, charging just enough above cost to make it worth their while to fill each room.

Using a combination of pricing strategies is called *hybrid pricing*, and is a key element in most successful businesses. The next part of this chapter explores ways to introduce hybrid pricing into your business, including premium products, no-frills products, package pricing and differential pricing.

Offering a premium product or service

With hybrid pricing, offering a premium product or service is only part of the picture. The idea is that as well as offering a premium product or service, you also offer a regular product or service. In other words, you target more than one type of customer.

Here are some examples:

- >> Amazon offers a range of different pricing for freight, depending on how quickly you want your order delivered.
- >> My butcher sells two types of minced beef: low-fat and not-so-low fat.
- >> The guy who mows our lawns offers two services: regular just-with-a-lawnmower mowing, and premium all-grass-edges-trimmed-within-an-inch-of-their-life mowing.

REMEMBER

Offering a premium product doesn't necessarily mean you compromise on the quality of your other products (a strategy that could risk your brand reputation). You can structure premiums in many different ways, such as faster service, guaranteed response time, additional services and complimentary extras.

Cutting back the frills

The flipside of premium pricing (refer to preceding section) is no-frills pricing. No-frills pricing doesn't necessarily mean inferior quality, but can include things such as off-peak pricing, lower service standards, longer response times, or limited availability. Here are some examples:

- >> Frequent-flyer programs place restrictions on what flights are available for frequent-flyer points.
- >> Many gyms offer low-cost membership if you attend outside peak periods.
- >> Tourism operators employ no-frills pricing for off-peak periods.

Have a think about how you could offer a no-frills service or no-frills product. Would this fit with your branding? How could you ensure that this pricing model doesn't undercut sales from your existing client base?

Getting creative with packages

Package pricing, where one product or service is bundled together with something else, is another example of hybrid pricing. Package pricing can include things such as bundling two or more products or services together, offering bonus products, and extended warranties.

Examples of package pricing include

>> A day spa offering a pedicure, waxing and massage as a package.

>> A tourism operator offering flights, accommodation and meals as a package.

>> A club offering a free giveaway of some kind for every membership renewal.

TIP

If you're just starting up a new business, you may be pushed to think of how you could offer package pricing. Keep thinking creatively. Keep in mind that your business doesn't need to provide all elements of the package and that often the best approach is to team up with another business.

Charging different prices for the same thing

Yet another pricing strategy — and one that sounds a little dodgy at first — is to charge different prices for the same thing (this is also known as *differential pricing*). Don't worry — I'm not proposing you breach trade guidelines and regulations. Instead, I'm talking about charging different prices depending on the quantity ordered, the total size of an order, the costs of shipping to customers, how promptly customers pay, how much the customer orders in the course of a year, and so on.

Differential pricing works really well for almost any business because it enables you to maintain your margins for regular sales, but generate extra income by selling to other customers at a discount.

Here are a few ways to implement differential pricing:

>> **Pricing based on customer location:** Charging different rates (either for shipping or for on-site service) depending on where the customer is located makes good sense, although you still want to keep your pricing structure pretty simple.

>> **Pricing based on loyalty:** Offering special pricing to customers who are members of your loyalty program or members of an affiliate organization is a good marketing strategy and rewards customer loyalty.

>> **Pricing based on order size or quantities ordered:** This kind of pricing makes intuitive sense straight off the bat. Almost any business will charge a different price for someone who buys 1,000 units rather than 10. (When you structure pricing according to quantity, this is called *quantity-break pricing*.)

>> **Pricing based on payment terms:** Offering credit terms is expensive, not just in terms of using up working capital but also because of the risk of bad debt. Consider offering higher discounts for payment upfront or payment within 7 days.

>> **Pricing based on total spending:** Providing reward incentives for total spending often features as part of loyalty programs and makes good business sense. For example, if customers spend more than $500 over the course of the year, they get something for free or a discount on their next purchase.

>> **Pricing based on customer commitment:** Another clever strategy is to offer discount pricing but make the customer jump through hoops to get it. Money-back coupons where you have to post proof of purchase to the supplier or price-match guarantees are examples of this kind of pricing.

Forming Your Final Plan of Attack

Previously in this chapter, I talk in detail about different pricing strategies. Thinking in this way may spark new ideas and creative thinking, but you might also feel a little overwhelmed and wonder where to start. So, here's my specific recommendation for the process to follow:

1. **Do some research as to what you think customers will be prepared to pay.**

   This research will involve looking at what competitors are charging as well as thinking about how your product or service is different and what value customers are likely to place on this difference.

2. **Think about how you could vary your product or service to provide two or three 'levels' of pricing (no-frills, regular and premium).**

   Not every business can offer multi-level pricing (for example, I don't know that I'd seek out a surgeon offering a no-frills service), but you'd be surprised how many types of businesses can. (Refer to the section 'Building a Hybrid-Pricing Plan', earlier in this chapter, for more on pricing levels.)

3. **Investigate at least two ways to bundle or package your offering with other products or services.**

   'Getting creative with packages', earlier in this chapter, provides a few ideas on this topic.

4. **Find two or three ways to charge your customers different prices for the same things.**

   This pricing strategy (differential pricing) is probably the most crucial of all. Even if you can't figure out how to have more than one level of pricing, or you can't come up with a method to create a package, you should be able to incorporate some form of differential pricing in your strategy. 'Charging different prices for the same thing', earlier in this chapter, provides some pointers as to how you can do this.

TIP

Although the upside of a hybrid pricing strategy is that you maximize the number of customers you can reach, and hopefully make premium profits on at least some of your sales, you can risk confusing customers if you offer too many options. As your business grows and changes, experiment with different pricing combinations to see what works best and gets the best response from your customers.

REMEMBER

Changing prices doesn't only mean raising prices. Always be open to new pricing plans, special offers, package pricing and so on. If you do decide to raise prices, try to do so incrementally and avoid big price hikes that may scare your customers. Alternatively, find ways to sneak price rises through the back door, such as only increasing prices on certain low-profile products or services, or getting rid of discounts.

ENSURING YOU VALUE YOURSELF AND YOUR TIME

When you first start a new enterprise, you probably can't charge for all the time you spend working on your business. After all, you're still setting up systems and building up goodwill in the first few months, testing what works and what doesn't, and trying to secure new customers.

However, once you've established a business model and started trading in earnest, it pays to monitor how many hours you're working. If you regularly spend upwards of 50 hours or so a week on your business and you're only yielding an average income, this may well indicate that your business model — and, by implication, your pricing structures — isn't working as well as they should.

Valuing your time properly also helps you to sell your business when you're ready to do so. When a business broker calculates how much a business is worth, they not only look at how much income the business generates, but also how many hours a week the owner(s) work. If the hourly rate generated by the business is low, the goodwill will probably be valued at zero, or even a negative amount.

Building Your Sales Forecast

Once you have figured out your pricing strategy (what you intend to charge per hour, per unit or per service rendered), the next step in your business plan is to create a sales forecast for the next 12 months (or, if your business hasn't started yet, create a sales forecast for the first 12 months of operation).

Creating sales forecasts prompts all kinds of questions. If you're charging by the hour, what's a reasonable number of hours to bill for each week? If you're selling items, how do you know how many you'll sell? What if you sell lots of different items, at different prices? In the following sections, I talk about the details behind creating this kind of projection.

Calculating hours in a working week

If your business charges by the hour or by the session (maybe you're a bookkeeper, consultant, counsellor, electrician, gardener, physiotherapist, plumber, private tutor, or some similar business), one of the first questions is how many hours can you reasonably charge for per week, per month, or per year.

Imagine a recent music graduate (I'll call her Maddie) wants to set up a business as a tutor. Maddie reckons she can teach about 48 students a week in lesson blocks of 30 minutes (that's 24 hours of teaching), and that she's going to charge $60 per hour. With this in mind, she reckons that she'll earn $74,880 per year. (That's 24 multiplied by 52 weeks multiplied by $60.)

Is Maddie correct in her estimate of income for the next 12 months? I'm going to test her calculations using the following step-by-step method, which you can use as well:

1. **Estimate how many days you're going to work each week, and how many hours you can realistically charge for each day to arrive at your average number of billable hours per week.**

When doing this calculation, remember to include billable hours only. Don't include travel time between locations, non-billable time due to administration/paperwork, or time spent running your business (bookkeeping, customer phone calls, marketing and so on).

2. **Estimate how much holiday you're going to take (or be forced to take) each year.**

Here, don't think in terms of lying on the beach watching the surf, but include both holidays where you go away and breaks where you may be available to work, but you can't. (For example, a school tutor probably won't get much work in school holidays, a gardener may find it hard to work in heavy rain or snow, or a consultant may find that work grinds to a halt before and after Christmas.)

In Table 8-1, I've included 12 weeks against the holiday Maddie will take annually, because that's the number of weeks of school holidays each year where she lives.

3. Make an allowance for public holidays.

Most people don't work public holidays. If you don't plan to (or maybe you can't because your customers will be unavailable), you have to allow for public holidays as well. Public holidays of ten days a year equates to an equivalent of two weeks per year. In Maddie's case, many public holidays also coincide with her local school holidays, so she only allows for five days (one week) of public holidays per year.

4. Think of what will happen if you get sick.

My observation is that being a freelancer is one of the best possible ways of ensuring good health. Knowing that you won't get paid if you don't show up is a real incentive to getting out the door, however you're feeling. However, most people do get sick from time to time, and it's realistic to make an allowance for this. In Maddie's case, she allows for five days (one week) of sick days per year.

5. Calculate how many weeks per year you will be able to charge for.

In Maddie's case (see Table 8-1), after taking out holidays, public holidays, and sick days, she can likely work a full week (that's 24 billable hours) for only 38 weeks of the year. (Most businesses that aren't dependent on school terms can probably work more weeks per year than this, however.)

6. Multiply the number of working weeks per year by the number of weekly billable hours, to arrive at your maximum billable hours per year.

As shown in Table 8-1, for Maddie this equals 38 weeks per year multiplied by 24 hours per week, making a total of 912 hours.

7. Multiply your maximum billable hours per year by your hourly rate.

The result for Maddie is $54,720 per year, quite different from her initial estimate of $74,880.

Note: The method shown in Table 8-1 only gives you the maximum billable hours per year for an example business that's up and running. If you're still getting your business established, not only will your calculations be very different but it also may be some time until you have enough customers to reach your maximum billable hours.

TABLE 8-1 **Calculating Maximum Billable Hours per Year**

Number of days worked per week	4
Average number of billable hours per day	6
Total billable hours per week	*24*
Number of holiday weeks per year	12
Number of public holidays per year, expressed in weeks	1
Number of sick days per year, expressed in weeks	1
Total working weeks per year	38
Maximum possible billable hours per year	**912**
Hourly rate	$60
Maximum possible income per year	*$54,720*

Increasing sales by hiring staff

If your business is primarily service-based, don't forget to think beyond your own time and how many hours you can pack into a week. Instead, expand your thinking to include delegating some of the work involved to employees or subcontractors.

Building a plan that involves employees servicing your customers (rather than just you servicing customers) is a vital part of any entrepreneurial conception. For example, don't just think of how many lawns you can mow, kids you can tutor, or companies you can consult to. Instead, picture a team of people mowing lawns, a whole school of tutors, or an entire posse of consultants.

REMEMBER

If your business is service-based, leveraging your expertise in this way is the only possible method by which you can hope to earn more than the industry average. For example, if you start up a business as a gardener, tutor, or physiotherapist, you can only work so many hours in the week. However, with a team of employees working for you, all delivering this service, you may be able to make a decent profit.

Predicting sales for a new business

If a business is still getting established, making an estimate of your first 12 months' sales can be really hard. However, to ensure your sales forecast is as realistic as possible, the more detail the better. Try to slice up sales targets by market segment, product, or region:

» **Market segment targets:** Market segment is a fancy word that really means type of customer or type of work. For example, a building contractor may split his market into new houses and renovations, a musician may split her market into weddings, private functions and pub gigs. A handyman may split his market into private clients and real estate agents.

» **Product-based targets:** Product-based targets work best if you sell products rather than services. You can set sales targets according to units sold, or dollars sold, of each product. For example, a car yard could aim to sell at least 20 cars a month, a real estate agent could try to sell five houses every month, and a lawnmowing business could set sales targets of 80 lawns per month.

» **Regional targets:** With regions, you set sales targets according to geographic regions. This works best for slightly larger businesses that typically have a dedicated salesperson or sales team in each region.

If you take on board any of the pricing strategy stuff I talk about earlier in this chapter (refer to the section 'Building a Hybrid-Pricing Plan' for more), chances are you're going to have a few different prices or packages on the go. Although this can make your sales forecast complicated, remember that the concept is simple: Try to incorporate a decent level of detail into initial sales estimates, including all items you sell or services you provide.

Predicting sales for an established business

If you've been running your business for a while, one of the most accurate ways of predicting sales is to analyze what sales have been for the last 12 months, and then build from there. Sure, you may have changed things — maybe you've switched to a new location, introduced new products or increased your pricing — but, nonetheless, your historical sales results are always going to provide you with the best indicator for future sales.

When basing sales forecasts on historical data, consider the following:

>> When looking at sales figures for previous months, check whether these figures are shown including or excluding sales/consumer tax. (Most salespeople think in terms of the final value of each sale; accountants tend to look at sales figures net of any taxes collected on behalf of the government.)

>> Does your business have significant seasonal variations? If so, have you factored these into your monthly forecasts?

>> If you examine the trends, is the business growing or declining? Ideally, you should analyze trends over two or more years to truly get a sense of what's happening.

>> Have any changes to pricing or product range occurred between last year and this year?

When looking at sales forecasts, also factor in personalities. Salespeople are often very buoyant with their predictions (this optimism tends to be part of the job), while accountants are typically gloom and doom. Hopefully, your business plan can arrive at a happy medium.

Creating Your Month-by-Month Forecast

At the simplest level, creating a forecast for the next 12 months can be as simple as listing the names of the months in one big row and writing an estimate underneath each one. However, this method is somewhat unsophisticated, to put it mildly.

One trick to improving the accuracy of sales forecasts is to maintain a good level of detail. Start by looking at your weekly sales forecasts (something I talk about earlier in this chapter in the section 'Building Your Sales Forecast') and extrapolate these figures to create monthly forecasts, bearing the following in mind:

>> If you've been thinking about your sales in terms of weeks, keep in mind that some months have four weeks and others have five.

>> Most business plans include sales projections for at least the next 12 months, if not 24 months.

>> You need to factor in holidays and other seasonal events. For example, unless you run a Santa Claus for hire business, Christmas and early January are quiet months for most businesses.

>> Show your sales before any consumer tax (sales tax, GST, VAT and so on) that you're obliged to charge to customers but have to then remit to the government.

TIP

>> If you run a service business and intend to deliver some services yourself, and some using contractors, consider separating the income that you generate, versus the income your contractors generate. Categorizing sales in this way helps you to be realistic about what you can achieve, demonstrates how much more income you can generate if you use subcontractors or employees, and also assists in calculating costs (a topic I cover in Chapter 9).

>> If your business is something that has been done before, do some research to check how realistic your forecasts are. Look at industry benchmarks (something I discuss in more detail in Chapter 10), talk to your accountant, chat to people already working in the industry, join online networking groups or go to industry conferences.

Chapter **9**

Calculating Costs and Gross Profit

The summer just past stretched into weeks of long, sunny days. The next-door kids, Callum and Rhys, hatched a plot to make homemade lemonade and sell it to thirsty passers-by. Most days I'd stop and buy a glass and the kids would happily announce how much profit they'd made so far. The school holidays were almost at a close the afternoon I bumped into their dad in the supermarket. He had a trolley piled high with lemons. 'This profit the boys are making is costing me a fortune', he laughed.

Chances are that such halcyon days belong only to childhood and that, in your business, you're going to have to be seriously realistic about what everything costs. No more lemons for free.

In this chapter, I talk about calculating the costs for each sale that you make, and how to relate these calculations to your gross profit margins. And I show you how to build on your sales projections to include these costs so that you can create a forecast of your gross profit for the year ahead. This forecast forms the basis of your Profit & Loss Projection, a report essential to any business plan.

Calculating the Cost of Each Sale

The focus of this chapter is the costs that go up and down in direct relation to your sales. For example, if you manufacture wooden tables, your costs include timber. If you sell books, your costs include the purchase of books from publishers.

If you run a small service-based business and you have no employees, you may find that you have no costs of this nature (and, hence, most of this chapter is irrelevant to you). However, before abandoning this chapter willy-nilly, do read through the first couple of sections ('Identifying your variable costs' and 'Costing your service'), just to make sure.

Identifying your variable costs

In order to complete the expenses part of your Profit & Loss Projection for the next 12 months in your business plan, you first need to grasp the difference between variable costs and fixed expenses. *Variable costs* (also sometimes called *direct costs* or *cost of goods sold*) are the costs that go up and down in direct relation to your sales.

This theory may seem all very well, but you need to understand how it applies in the context of your own business. Here are some examples that may help:

>> If you're a manufacturer, variable costs are the materials you use in order to make things, such as raw materials and production labor. (For the boys next door making lemonade, their variable costs were lemons and sugar.)

>> If you're a retailer, your main variable cost is the costs of the goods you buy to resell to customers. Other variable costs, particularly for online retailers, may include packaging and postage.

>> If you're a service business, you may not have any variable costs, but possible variable costs include sales commissions, booking fees, equipment rental, guest consumables, or employee/subcontract labor.

Fixed expenses (also sometimes called *indirect costs* or *overheads*) are expenses that stay constant, regardless of whether your sales go up and down. Typical fixed expenses for your business may include accounting fees, bank fees, computer expenses, electricity, insurance, motor vehicles, rental, stationery, and wages.

TIP

Not sure which variable costs apply to your business? Figure 9-1 provides a question-based checklist to prompt you to think about your business and what variable costs it may have.

IDENTIFYING VARIABLE COSTS FOR YOUR BUSINESS

Do you use raw materials to create new products?
Examples: Ingredients, foods, timber, metals, plastics, paper

Do you purchase finished products or materials for resale?
Examples: A clothes shop buys clothes, a cafe buys coffee beans, and a landscaper buys soil and plants

Do you purchase any materials for packaging?
Examples: Cardboard, bubble wrap, bottles, caps, envelopes

Do you use any energy as part of manufacturing items?
Examples: Electricity or gas in the factory

Do you employ any labor when manufacturing items?
Examples: Factory wages, subcontractor wages, production wages

Do you use employees or subcontractors to deliver services to your customers?
Examples: An electrical contractor employs electricians; a gardener employs laborers.

Do you pay any commissions on sales?
Examples: Sales commission, sales bonuses, sales rebates, sales discounts

Do you have any expenses relating to importing goods from overseas?
Examples: Inwards shipping costs, customs fees, external storage costs

Do you have costs relating to distributing or shipping items?
Examples: Outwards freight, couriers, warehouse rent, warehouse staff

---

FIGURE 9-1: Identifying variable costs for your business.

Costing your service

I mention near the beginning of this chapter that if you're providing a service, you may not have any variable costs associated with your business. However, you may well have some minor costs associated with providing your service and, as soon as your business grows, you will have the cost of hiring employees or contractors to provide the service on behalf of your business.

Table 9-1 shows some examples where variable costs apply.

TABLE 9-1 **Variable Costs Examples for Service Businesses**

Type of Business	Likely Variable Costs
Contract cleaning	Cleaning staff wages, cleaning materials
Holiday house	Guest consumables, booking commissions
Massage therapist	Daily room hire
Home maintenance business	Building materials, cost of subcontractors
Medical practitioner	Medical supplies, pathology

TIP

If you're unsure whether something is a variable cost or a fixed expense, ask yourself this: Do you spend more on this item as sales increase? If your answer is yes, chances are this item is a variable cost.

Costing items that you buy and sell

When calculating costs for items that you buy and then sell you have two types of costs to consider:

>> **Incoming costs:** These are the costs involved in getting the goods to your door. Incoming costs often include freight and, for importers, may also include customs charges, duties and tax. Incoming costs may also vary significantly depending on the quantity you order.

>> **Outgoing costs:** These are the costs involved in making the sale and getting the goods to your customer. Outgoing costs include e-commerce fees, merchant fees, outwards freight, packaging and storage.

In Table 9-2, I show a costings worksheet for a wholesaler. You can see that, at first glance, the wholesaler's buy price is $9.00 and the sell price is $18.00, making for a handsome margin of 50 percent. Browse through the figures in more detail, however, allowing for freight, storage, commissions and so on, and you can see that the final margin is something much closer to a paltry 24 percent. (For more on gross profit and gross profit margins, see the section 'Understanding Gross Profit', later in this chapter.)

TABLE 9-2 Calculating True Costs and Margins

Description	Percentage of Sell Price	$
Sell Price (Before Taxes)		**$18.00**
Less **Variable Costs**		
Buy price for this item	50%	$9.00
Inwards freight to warehouse	5%	$0.90
Storage costs warehouse	2%	$0.36
E-commerce fees	10%	$1.80
Outwards freight to customer	8%	$1.44
Packaging	1%	$0.18
Total costs of selling		**$13.68**
Gross Profit		**$4.32**
Gross Profit Margin	*24%*	

Creating product costings for manufacturers

If you manufacture products, one of the most crucial steps in your business plan is to create an accurate costing worksheet for each product that you sell. This process can be pretty tedious, but without knowing exactly what everything costs, you can't move forward and plan.

Table 9-3 shows an example product costing and the kind of information to include. I've taken this example from one of the businesses I've mentored — a family member who started a business making homemade gourmet sauces.

TIP

Can you see how the example in Table 9-3 puts a value on labor? You may think this doesn't apply to you, because chances are if you're just starting out in business, you're contributing your own labor for free. However, when creating a product costing, you're best to include a realistic allowance for how much the labor would cost if you were to pay for someone else to create the product. This way, you can see the 'true' profitability of each product, and you get a better sense of the long-term potential of your enterprise.

TABLE 9-3 Cost of Producing One Bottle of Pickle

Item	$	Notes
100g fresh tomato	$0.80	Based on seasonal average
30g onion	$0.05	
20g sugar	$0.03	Based on buying in bulk 50kg bags
5g salt	$0.01	Based on buying in bulk 10kg bags
Cost of labor	$0.88	Average 400 bottles per day, with labor $350 per day
Kitchen rental	$0.38	Average 400 bottles per day, with rental $150 per day
Bottle plus lid	$0.45	
Label	$0.35	
Packaging	$0.40	$3.20 per custom box, 8 bottles per box
Total	$3.35	

The other interesting thing to consider is volume discounts. For example, in the product shown in Table 9-3, the cost of sugar is based on buying 50 kilograms at a time. However, how much would this business save if the owner was able to buy 100 kilograms at a time? (Even if your business can't afford to buy in large quantities yet, just knowing that your costs may reduce dramatically as your business grows is an important part of the business planning process.)

Understanding Gross Profit

You've almost certainly heard of the terms *gross profit* or *gross profit margins* but are you entirely clear what these terms mean and why an understanding of these terms is so crucial to your business plan? If you have even a moment's hesitation in answering 'yes' to this question, then read on . . .

Calculating gross profit

Put simply, gross profit is equal to sales less variable costs. A few examples may help bring this concept to life:

>> A clothing retailer buys a skirt from the wholesaler for $20 and sells it for $50. Their gross profit is $30.

>> A massage therapist charges $80 per massage but the therapy center takes $25 as a booking and room fee. Their gross profit is $55.

>> A carpenter charges $800 for fixing a veranda. Materials cost $200 and labor for their apprentice costs $100. Their gross profit is $500.

Sounds okay so far? Just bear in mind:

>> Gross profit equals sales less variable costs.

>> Gross profit is always more than net profit.

>> The more you sell, the more gross profit you make.

Figuring gross profit margins

Following on from the examples in the preceding section, if a clothing retailer buys a skirt for $20 and sells it for $50, the gross profit is $30. Sounds easy, but how do I figure out the gross profit margin? As follows:

Gross profit margin = gross profit divided by sales multiplied by 100

In this example, the retailer's gross profit margin equals $30 divided by $50 (that's gross profit divided by sales) multiplied by 100, which is 60 percent.

As I mention earlier, the more you sell, the more gross profit you make. However, if your costs stay constant, your gross profit margin stays the same, regardless of how much you sell. For example, if this retailer sells four skirts, their sales would be $200, their costs would be $80, their gross profit would be $120, but their gross profit margin would still be the same, at 60 percent.

Table 9-4 shows the gross profit and gross profit margins for the three examples from the preceding section.

Unless you know that something cost more to buy or to make than what you sold it for, both your gross profit and your gross profit margin should always be a positive figure.

TABLE 9-4 Calculating Gross Profit and Gross Profit Margin

	Clothing Retailer	Massage Therapist	Carpenter
Sell price	$50.00	$80.00	$800.00
Costs	$20.00	$25.00	$300.00
Gross Profit	$30.00	$55.00	$500.00
Gross Profit Margin	60%	69%	63%

Looking at margins over time

So far in this chapter, the examples I use talk about gross profit per unit sold or hour worked. However, in real life gross profit margins often vary from one transaction to the next (shopkeepers make a higher margin on gourmet jams than they do on milk, for example).

For this reason, it's good to be able to calculate your average gross profit margins over a period of time. Here's how some different kinds of businesses go about calculating their gross profit:

>> A builder constructs a house that then sells for $500,000. He spends $360,000 on materials and labor to build this house. His gross profit on the job is $140,000, and his gross profit margin is 28 percent.

>> A couple making homemade chili sauce that they sell in all different shapes and sizes, and at different prices, can see that they made $80,000 in sales over the last 12 months and spent $20,000 on ingredients, bottles, labelling and freight. Their gross profit for the year is $60,000, and their average gross profit margin is 75 percent.

>> A teenager buys secondhand clothes and resells them online. Last month, they sold $2,500 and spent $1,300 on buying clothes and postage. Their gross profit for the month is $1,200, and their average gross profit margin is 48 percent.

Analyzing Margins for Your Own Business

Have you been reading this chapter and thinking to yourself that this theory is all very well, but you're not a retailer, a carpenter, or a massage therapist? If so, never fear. In the following sections, I explain how to apply the principles of gross and net profit to your own business.

Calculating margins when you charge by the hour

If you have a service business and you charge by the hour, calculating your gross profit can be blindingly easy. Why? Because sometimes, a service business has no variable costs, and gross profit equals 100 percent of income. Read on to find out more.

Here's how you work out your gross profit and gross profit margin if you have a service business:

1. **Write down your hourly charge-out rate, not including any taxes that you charge to customers (such as GST, VAT, or sales tax).**

2. **Ask yourself whether any variable costs are associated with your service and, if so, calculate how much these costs are per hour.**

    The most likely cost for a service business is employees or subcontract labor. For example, when I ran a contract bookkeeping service, I paid my contractors an hourly rate for doing bookkeeping. This was a variable cost associated with my service.

    If you're a sole owner-operator with no employees, you may find that no variable costs are associated with your service.

3. **Subtract the cost you calculated in Step 2 from the hourly rate from Step 1.**

    This is your gross profit for this service. If you have no variable costs associated with your service, your hourly gross profit is the same as your hourly charge-out rate.

4. **Divide the gross profit you calculated in Step 3 by the hourly rate from Step 1, and divide your result by 100.**

    If you have no variable costs associated with your service, your gross profit margin will be 100 percent.

5. Consider the profitability of your service model.

Most service businesses need a decent gross profit margin in order to survive. If you're subcontracting out your services, don't underestimate the margin you'll need in order to cover all your business expenses. For example, if you're charging customers $100 per hour but paying employees $70 per hour, leaving yourself with a slim gross profit margin of 30 percent, you're almost certainly going to be doing things tough if this is your only income.

Calculating margins when you sell products

If you buy or manufacture items that you sell to others, each item has a separate gross profit margin. If you use accounting software to track your inventory, you'll be able to generate reports that calculate gross profit margins for you. However, if you don't have this resource, grab a calculator and work through the following for each item you sell:

1. Write down the sell price of this item, not including any taxes that you charge to customers (such as GST, VAT, or sales tax).

If the sell price varies depending on the customer, do the analysis for each price you sell this item for.

2. Write down the cost of this item.

If you buy this item from someone else, write down the total cost of purchasing this item, including freight but not including any taxes that you can claim back from the government (such as GST or VAT). If you manufacture this item, write down the total cost of all materials and production labor.

3. Subtract the cost you calculated in Step 2 from the sell price you calculated in Step 1.

This is your gross profit for this item.

4. Divide the gross profit you calculated in Step 3 by the sell price you calculated in Step 1, and divide your result by 100.

5. Consider the results and your fate in life.

Number crunching is not an end in itself. Does this margin seem reasonable? If you're not sure, ask around other people who work in the same industry as yourself, and try to get a sense of what margins you should expect.

Always bear in mind that, so long as your pricing policies remain consistent, your gross profit margin should stay relatively constant, no matter how much you sell.

Calculating margins if you do big projects

If you do lots of big projects over the course of a year — maybe you're a builder, you do custom manufacturing or you do big contract consultancy jobs — you're going to find it tricky to calculate your hourly gross profit, or your gross profit per unit sold. A different tack is required:

1. **Look at your total sales for 12 months, not including any taxes charged to the customer (such as GST or VAT).**

   I'm talking about total sales for all the different products that you sell, combined. If you're looking at a Profit & Loss report to get this figure, don't include things such as interest income, or sundry income from services.

2. **Add up your total variable costs for 12 months, not including any consumer tax paid (such as GST or VAT).**

   If you're an owner-operator with no employees running a service business, you may find that no variable costs are associated with your service. Otherwise, if you're unsure how to figure out what your variable costs are, refer to 'Identifying your variable costs', earlier in this chapter.

3. **Subtract the total costs you calculated in Step 2 from the total sales you calculated in Step 1.**

   This is your gross profit for the past 12 months.

4. **Divide the gross profit you calculated in Step 3 by the total sales you calculated in Step 1, and divide your result by 100.**

5. **Review your overall profitability.**

   What makes an acceptable gross profit margin varies from business to business. However, what's important for you is to be aware of your gross profit margin and ensure that it stays consistent over time.

Building Your Gross Profit Projection

In the earlier chapters in this book, I talk about clarifying your business idea and competitive strategies (Chapters 2 and 3), creating a budget for start-up expenses (Chapter 7), and setting prices and creating your first sales projection (Chapter 8). Next on the road map is expanding your sales projection to add an estimate of direct costs so that you can arrive at a projection of your gross profit for the next 12 months.

Note: I'm assuming here that you've already made a stab at predicting sales for the next 12 months. If you haven't, scoot back to Chapter 8 to complete this process. What you're aiming for is a monthly estimate of total sales for the next 12 months. This could be a single total for each month, or you may choose to split sales into several categories (similar to the first few rows of Figure 9-2).

	A	B	C	D	E	F	G
1		Price	Materials	Labor			
2	Flip Out Package	$ 350.00	$ 45.00	$ 175.00			
3	Trees About Package	$ 490.00	$ 60.00	$ 175.00			
4	Adventure Package	$ 650.00	$ 85.00	$ 240.00			
5							
6	**Total Parties Sold Using Owner's Labor**	Jul	Aug	Sep	Oct	Nov	Dec
7	Flip Out Package	8	8	8	8	8	8
8	Trees About Package	4	4	4	4	4	4
9	Adventure Package	2	1	1	1	1	1
10							
11	**Total Parties Sold Using Subcontract or Employee Labor**						
12	Flip Out Package	12	12	13	8	12	12
13	Trees About Package	8	6	8	10	12	12
14	Adventure Package	2	3	4	4	5	4
15							
16	**Income Generated**	Jul	Aug	Sep	Oct	Nov	Dec
17	Sales - Flip Out Package	$ 7,000	$ 7,000	$ 7,350	$ 5,600	$ 7,000	$ 7,000
18	Sales - Trees About Package	$ 5,880	$ 4,900	$ 5,880	$ 6,860	$ 7,840	$ 7,840
19	Sales - Adventure Package	$ 2,600	$ 2,600	$ 3,250	$ 3,250	$ 3,900	$ 3,250
20	**Total Sales**	$ 15,480	$ 14,500	$ 16,480	$ 15,710	$ 18,740	$ 18,090
21							
22	**Variable Costs**						
23	Materials & Labor - Flip Out Package	$ 3,000	$ 3,000	$ 3,220	$ 2,120	$ 3,000	$ 3,000
24	Materials & Labor - Trees About Package	$ 2,120	$ 1,650	$ 2,120	$ 2,590	$ 3,060	$ 3,060
25	Materials & Labor - Adventure Package	$ 820	$ 1,060	$ 1,385	$ 1,385	$ 1,710	$ 1,385
26	**Total Cost of Sales**	$ 5,940	$ 5,710	$ 6,725	$ 6,095	$ 7,770	$ 7,445
27							
28	**Gross Profit**	$ 9,540	$ 8,790	$ 9,755	$ 9,615	$ 10,970	$ 10,645

FIGURE 9-2: Building a gross profit projection for a service with employees or subcontractors.

What you do next depends on what kind of business you're working on.

Simply you

This type of business has the simplest of financial forecasts. Simply enter the heading 'Variable Costs' and leave the figures in this row blank. However, note that if you forecast substantial growth for your business, you may not be able to do all the work yourself, and you may need to hire subcontractors or use employee labor. In which case, you'll need to show the variable costs of this labor (read on to find out more . . .).

Adding little helpers

If you have a service business and you use employee or sub-contract labor, complete your sales projections for the next 12 months, but separate out sales where you're doing to do the work, and sales where you'll get employees or subcontractors to do the work, similar to Figure 9-2.

Small-scale productions

For this kind of business, I'm talking about someone who buys or manufactures a few specific products and then resells them. Examples could include someone making homemade jams, a baker selling pastries, a café selling a limited range of items or a cabinet-maker producing a limited range of furniture.

To create a gross profit projection for this kind of business, first complete your sales projections for the next 12 months, with a separate row for each product, and then list your variable costs for the same period, again using a separate row for each product. Add a row that calculates gross profit (sales less cost of sales), and that's all there is to it.

More in the mix

Sometimes, the idea with variable costs is that they are a stable percentage of income. For example, if you pay commissions on sales, these commissions are normally a certain percentage. Or if you're a retailer, the cost of the goods you buy is probably a similar percentage of sales each time you make a sale.

If your variable costs are always a pretty stable percentage of sales, the trick is to set up your gross profit projection so that your variable costs calculate automatically. In other words, set up your worksheet so that if you increase sales, variable costs automatically increase as well.

For example, in Figure 9-3, the bookseller knows that for every $100 of full-price books he sells, it costs him $60 to buy the books. In other words, his variable costs represent 60 percent of sales. Similarly, he knows that remainder books cost him, on average, 20 percent of the sale value.

	A	B	C	D	E	F	G
		Average Sell Price	Cost as a % of sales				
1							
2	Full-price books	$ 24.99	60%				
3	Remainder books	$ 19.99	20%				
4	Gift and other products	$ 17.99	65%				
5							
6							
7		Jul	Aug	Sep	Oct	Nov	Dec
8	Full-price books sales	$ 25,000	$ 25,750	$ 26,500	$ 27,500	$ 35,000	$ 45,800
9	Remainder book sales	$ 15,000	$ 15,450	$ 15,900	$ 16,500	$ 21,000	$ 27,480
10	Gifts & other sales	$ 2,750	$ 2,833	$ 2,915	$ 3,025	$ 3,850	$ 5,038
11	TOTAL SALES	$ 42,750	$ 44,033	$ 45,315	$ 47,025	$ 59,850	$ 78,318
12							
13							
14	Purchases full-price books	$ 15,000	$ 15,450	$ 15,900	$ 16,500	$ 21,000	$ 27,480
15	Purchases remainders	$ 3,000	$ 3,090	$ 3,180	$ 3,300	$ 4,200	$ 5,496
16	Purchases gifts	$ 1,788	$ 1,841	$ 1,895	$ 1,966	$ 2,503	$ 3,275
17	TOTAL VARIABLE COSTS	$ 19,788	$ 20,381	$ 20,975	$ 21,766	$ 27,703	$ 36,251
18							
19	GROSS PROFIT	$ 22,963	$ 23,651	$ 24,340	$ 25,259	$ 32,148	$ 42,067

FIGURE 9-3: Building a gross profit projection for a business selling lots of different kinds of products, or calculating costs on a percentage basis.

You can create a gross profit projection similar to Figure 9-3 by first listing sales, then listing variable costs (which you calculate as a percentage of sales), and then calculating gross profit (which will be sales less variable costs). Easy!

TIP

Can you see how I show the average cost of sales as a percentage in the top of the worksheet in Figure 9-3? The neat thing about working in this way is that if I change one of these percentages, my variable costs change automatically too. In addition, working in this way enables me to experiment with different scenarios. For example, imagine that this is your business and you're thinking of switching suppliers. The service is much better, but the cost of books from this supplier will be 65 percent of sales, rather than 60 percent. By changing one figure in the top of your worksheet, you can see instantly the impact this change would make to your profitability.

Chapter **10**

Managing Expenses

Although a business plan takes many shapes and sizes, pretty much every business plan includes a projection of both income and expenses for the next 12 months ahead. (Some business plans extend further than this, for three or even five years; however, for most purposes, 12 months usually does just fine.)

In this chapter, I focus on the expenses element of this 12-month forecast. Estimating future expenses isn't some idle form of crystal-ball gazing where you pluck some figures out of the air until you arrive at a final prediction of profit that makes you sleep easy. Instead, planning each expense in detail provides you with an opportunity for a reality check, even if this reality can prove rather chilling at times.

In this chapter, I suggest that if you're creating your first business plan, you look at your personal expenses as well. After all, in the absence of benevolent fairy godmothers or inheritances from wealthy great-aunties, starting a business that requires your full-time input but doesn't generate enough profits for you to survive is never going to fly.

Concentrating on Expenses

I accept that this book provides no gripping plot, murders, or sex scenes, and that few people picking up this book are going to start at Chapter 1 and read through to the end. Instead, you'll probably flick through the pages, picking and choosing the bits you're interested in, which is generally okay. However, when you're working on financial projections, simply jumping in at whatever chapter catches your eye can be a time-wasting exercise.

As outlined through this book, the typical financial planning cycle involves creating a start-up budget, followed by estimating prices, costs, and expenses. You then use this information to create Profit & Loss Projections, break-even analysis reports and Cashflow Projections.

If you've been working through this cycle chapter by chapter, you'll be over halfway through this process. (Chapter 7 focuses on budgeting for start-up expenses, Chapter 8 on prices and rates, Chapter 9 on product costs and gross profit and Chapter 10 — that's this chapter — on expense budgets. Chapter 11 then completes the financial planning process.)

So, if you've just picked up this book and plunged in at this chapter, pause for a moment and check that you've already covered the initial stages of your financial plan (that is, creating a start-up budget, setting prices and calculating product costs). If you haven't, take the time to get these foundations in place first.

Separating start-up expenses and variable costs from ongoing expenses

When planning for business expenses, always separate start-up expenses from ongoing expenses:

>> *Start-up expenses* are one-off expenses that you encounter when you first start a business, such as new equipment, company formation expenses, legal expenses and signage. I talk lots about start-up expenses in Chapter 7.

>> *Ongoing expenses* are the kind of expenses that occur year in and year out, and which form a regular part of everyday trading. Ongoing expenses are the focus of the next part of this chapter.

When you're working with Profit & Loss Projections in your business plan, you only include ongoing expenses. Start-up expenses — if relevant to you — are shown separately.

Similarly, remember the difference between variable costs and fixed expenses.

>> *Variable costs* (also sometimes called *direct costs* or *cost of goods sold*) are the costs that go up and down in direct relation to your sales.

>> *Fixed expenses* (also sometimes called *indirect costs* or *overheads*) are expenses that stay constant, regardless of whether your sales go up and down.

This chapter focuses on fixed expenses only. For more about creating a worksheet that forecasts variable costs, refer to Chapter 9.

Thinking of what expenses to include

If you've been running your business for a while, you already have a good idea of what your expenses are going to be. However, if you're just getting started with your business plan, thinking of the types of expenses you may encounter can be tricky. Are you going to take out insurance? What about accounting fees? Will you need to pay any professional memberships? What expenses could you face that you haven't even thought of yet?

TIP

Figure 10-1 shows a Business Expenses worksheet that lists expenses in the first column, how often they occur in the second column, an estimate of the amount in the third, and a monthly estimate in the fourth. To create a Business Expenses worksheet similar to this one, here's what to do:

1. **Open up a new worksheet in Excel or Google Sheets and list business expenses in the first column, followed by the months of the year in the first row.**

    Remember to only include ongoing business expenses at this point, and not variable costs or start-up expenses. For the months of the year, you're usually best to project at least 12 months ahead. (I only show six months in Figure 10-1 due to lack of space.)

2. **Estimate the amount of each expense, and in a separate column, specify whether this expense occurs weekly, fortnightly, quarterly, monthly, or annually. Show all amounts exclusive of value-added tax (such as GST or VAT).**

   If you haven't started trading yet and you're still creating a business plan, estimating expenses can be very tricky. See 'Using AI to Secure Business Intelligence', later in this chapter, for ways to improve the accuracy of your estimates.

   If your business is already trading, the best way to make estimates is to look at what you've spent in the past. Supplier invoices and Profit & Loss Statements are all good sources for this information.

   Round all amounts to the nearest $100 or so — forecasts aren't meant to be an exact science.

3. **Based on the frequency of this expense, enter monthly estimates for each one.**

WARNING

   Be super careful with any expenses that you pay weekly. For example, if you rent is, say, $500 a week, your monthly budget is not four times this amount. To calculate a monthly budget for something you pay weekly, you need to first multiply the weekly amount by 52, and then divide it by 12. In this example, $500 a week rent multiplied by 52 equals $26,000. Divide this by 12 and you get just over $2,166 a month (not $2,000).

   For more about showing weekly or irregular expenses, see 'Allowing for irregular payments', later in this chapter.

4. **Think carefully about the timing of any expenses you pay only quarterly or annually.**

   For example, Figure 10-1 only shows a single amount in February for accounting fees, because these are only paid once a year.

5. **Review the totals in the Total Expenses row.**

   The Total Expenses row should automatically add up the rows above it. This means that if you change a figure, the total recalculates automatically. In Excel, the easiest way to do this is to press your AutoSum button (the one with a Greek symbol that looks a bit like an 'E').

6. Save your work and ponder.

With your final worksheet complete, spend a generous amount of time checking it over, ensuring it makes sense and is realistic.

	A	B	C	F	G	H	I	J	K
	Type of Expense	Freqency	Estimate Per Period	Jan	Feb	Mar	Apr	May	Jun
1									
2	Accounting Fees	Annually	$2,000	$0	$2,000	$0	$0	$0	$0
3	Bank Charges	Monthly	$100	$100	$100	$100	$100	$100	$100
4	Communication Expenses	Monthly	$380	$380	$380	$380	$380	$380	$380
5	Consultant Expenses	Quarterly	$300	$300	$300	$300	$300	$300	$300
6	Insurance	Monthly	$280	$280	$280	$280	$280	$280	$280
7	Interest Expense	Monthly	$520	$520	$520	$520	$520	$520	$520
8	IT Expenses	Monthly	$450	$450	$450	$450	$450	$450	$450
9	Lease Expenses	Monthly	$800	$800	$800	$800	$800	$800	$800
10	Marketing Expenses	Annually	$14,400	$1,200	$1,200	$1,200	$1,200	$1,200	$1,200
11	Merchant Fees	Monthly	$1,200	$621	$709	$823	$729	$945	$964
12	Motor Vehicle Expenses	Monthly	$350	$350	$350	$350	$350	$1,800	$350
13	Office Supplies	Annually	$1,800	$150	$150	$150	$150	$150	$150
14	Rental Expense	Fortnightly	$1,500	$3,250	$3,250	$3,250	$3,250	$3,250	$3,250
15	Repairs and Maintenance	Annually	$6,000	$500	$500	$500	$500	$500	$500
16	Staff Amenities	Monthly	$300	$300	$300	$300	$300	$300	$300
17	Travel Expenses	Monthly	$350	$350	$350	$350	$350	$350	$350
18	Utilities	Quarterly	$2,400	$600	$0	$0	$600	$0	$0
19	Wages and Salaries	Weekly	$900	$3,600	$3,600	$4,500	$3,600	$3,600	$4,500
20	Wages oncosts	Weekly	$108	$540	$540	$675	$540	$540	$675
21	Total Expenses			$14,291	$15,779	$14,928	$14,399	$15,465	$15,069

FIGURE 10-1: Forecasting expenses for the months ahead.

Fine-tuning Your Worksheet

With the first draft of your expenses worksheet complete, you're ready to fine-tune it so you can be sure that your projections are as accurate as possible. Look at relationships between expenses, think about irregular payments, and focus on large expenses in a bit more detail.

Recognizing relationships

Are any of your expense categories directly related to one another? For example, staff oncosts usually go up or down in direct proportion to wages.

TIP

The trick is to tell your spreadsheet about relationships so that it calculates them for you automatically. In Figure 10-1, for example, you can see a figure for wages in Row 19. I know that wages oncosts average 15 percent of wages, so my formula for wages oncosts in January is =F19*15%. The neat thing about specifying relationships in this way is that when you change one figure in the spreadsheet, other figures change automatically, too.

Allowing for irregular payments

When creating expense projections, take a while to consider expenses that vary from month to month or change with the seasons. Here are a few specifics to consider:

>> Utility bills, such as electricity and gas, often fall due every two or three months, rather than every month.

>> If you pay wages every week, bear in mind that every third month you'll get a month with five paydays, not four.

>> Think about seasonal variations. Depending on your business, expenses can increase or decrease dramatically at different times of year.

>> If you're a small owner-operated business, think about when you may take holidays, and whether you need to increase your wages expense during this time.

>> If you don't know when an expense will fall due, you can average this expense across the year. For example, I know that my car usually clocks in at approximately $2,000 of repairs per year, but I never know when these bills are going to fall due. With these kinds of expenses, I just use my annual estimate and leave a monthly amount in place.

Playing the 10 percent rule

I have a technique that I've developed over the years as a way of ensuring that my expense estimates are more likely to be accurate. What I do is go through the worksheet and identify any expenses that make up around 10 percent, or more, of the total expenses. For example, if you look at Figure 10-1, you can see that marketing expenses make up almost 10 percent of total expenses each month. For such a small business, this expense makes up a significant proportion of outgoings.

TIP

Next, for any expense that makes up around 10 percent of total expenses, I see if it makes sense to dissect this expense in more detail. In the example shown in Figure 10-1, I would suggest to the business that they add more detail about marketing expense in the worksheet — for example, listing different types of marketing expenditure separately.

Securing Business Intelligence

You can find out how other businesses in your industry are faring by using something called *business benchmarking*. Business benchmarking results are compiled using survey results from other business owners. Individual results are always kept confidential, and it's only the averages (or highs and lows) that are reported, as well as percentages. For example, if I'm planning to open a boutique bar and I'm working on my business plan, I could look at the benchmarks for bars and clubs and see what percentage of sales I could expect to spend on alcohol, food, rental, wages and so on, or how much profit an average bar in a city suburb makes each year.

TIP

Business benchmarks provide an excellent way for you to check whether your financial projections are realistic, especially if you haven't started your business yet.

Locating benchmarks for your business

How best to locate benchmarks for your business depends on your location and industry. A good starting point for resources is to ask AI (using ChatGPT or a similar tool). For example, you might ask 'Where can I find business benchmarks for an auto-mechanic business in the UK?' or 'How can I find business benchmarks for a café in regional Australia?' or 'What gross profit does an average physiotherapist business in North America make?'

You can also find benchmarks from a few other sources:

>> **Banks:** Banks often have industry-specific information useful for benchmarking.

>> **Benchmarking services:** Search online using the word 'benchmarks' or 'benchmarking' to find organizations specializing in the collation and resale of benchmarking data. IBISWorld and Statista are two of the best known services providing industry-wide reports and data. If your business is based in Australia, Benchmarking Data & Research (www.benchmarking.com.au) also sell benchmarking data.

>> **The 'big 5' accounting practices:** The major accounting and consulting firms, such as KPMG, PWC, or EY, usually publish reports on key industries that are available for a fee. Call to find out what reports are available for your industry.

>> **Boutique accounting practices:** Some accountants specialize in particular industries. For example, I know of someone who has a boutique accountancy practice specializing in medical practitioners and dentists. Specialist accountants will be very conversant with their industry and can quickly advise you whether your financial projections fall within industry standards.

>> **Government departments:** Government departments such as the Bureau of Economic Analysis (US) or Companies House (UK) can be a great resource; Companies House in particular allows you to view filed accounts for any registered UK company. The Canadian government is also a great resource (search for 'Government of Canada, financial performance data').

>> **Industry associations:** Industry associations almost always have some reference materials regarding benchmarks and are usually willing to advise members.

>> **Networking meetings:** If you have colleagues working in the same industry but not in direct competition (maybe you're all in professional practice of some kind but specializing in different areas), you may find these colleagues are willing to share information regarding rent, wages, or other expenses as a percentage of sales. (However, most business owners will be reticent regarding the actual amount paid for these items.)

Using benchmarks as part of your plan

With a topic such as benchmarking, I like to use a detailed example to bring the whole concept to life.

In this fictional example, imagine a doctor (I'll call her Kate) has recently opened a new medical practice. As part of her business plan, she has purchased a set of benchmarks from a benchmarking organization (see Table 10-1).

In Table 10-1, you can see that the average medical practice has a turnover of $822,000. The lowest practice in the survey has a turnover of $274,600 and the highest has a turnover of $1,691,500. Sounds interesting enough, but the really practical aspects for you — in planning your business — are the percentages. For example, can you see that the average medical practice spends 25.3 percent on wages and 5.5 percent of turnover on rent?

TABLE 10-1 Using Business Benchmarks

Indicator	Average	Low	High
Total income (thousands)	$822.2	$274.6	$1,691.5
Drugs, supplies, consumables	2.16%	0.76%	3.59%
Wages and salaries (staff only, not owners)	25.30%	15.10%	39.34%
Rent of premises	5.52%	1.92%	9.09%
Staff oncosts	2.23%	1.11%	3.87%
Non-vehicle depreciation/lease/hire purchase	2.70%	0.56%	5.18%
Net profit	49.22%	30.21%	67.31%
Support staff per practitioner	1.52	1.00	2.35
Average consult length (minutes)	15	10	19
Average no. of consults per doctor per week	156	105	200
Opening hours per day	9.51	8.00	11.00
Opening days per week	5.50	5.00	6.10

Now look at Figure 10-2, which shows Kate's first year's Profit & Loss report. Can you see how in column C, Kate has calculated how much each expense is as a percentage of sales? For example, her rent at $18,200 per year is 6.4 percent of income (that's $18,200 divided by $285,000 multiplied by 100). Compare this rent against other medical practices, and you can see that Kate is paying slightly above the average rent of 5.5 percent. Similarly, Kate is spending 32.6 percent on wages, well above the average of 25.3 percent.

You may be wondering how to apply the preceding example to your own business — after all, chances are that you're not a medical practitioner. Here's what to do:

1. **Complete your sales, cost of sales and expenses projection for the next 12 months.**

For more detail on how to do these projections, refer to the first part of this chapter, along with Chapters 8 and 9. Alternatively, if your business has already been trading for a while, you could generate a Profit & Loss report for the most recent 12 months of trading, and send this report to a spreadsheet.

2. **Add a column for % of sales, and create a formula for % of sales against each row.**

   Can you see the column of percentages in Figure 10-2? You can create this column by inserting a formula against the first cost of sales row and then copying this formula to all the other rows. For example, the formula that I type in cell C4 (next to Drugs, supplies, consumables) is '=B4/B2'. (The dollar signs in B2 mean you can copy this formula to other rows and the cell reference stays the same.) I then click the % button on my menu bar to show this figure as a percentage.

3. **Get hold of benchmarks for your industry.**

   I talk about how to find benchmarks earlier in this chapter (refer to 'Locating benchmarks for your business').

4. **Compare your business plan against the industry averages.**

   For example, if you're running a café and benchmarks show that the average cafe spends 30 percent on wages, compare this percentage with your projections and see whether you're spending, relatively speaking, more or less.

You may find it tricky to find benchmarks that are relevant to you. Maybe you've invented a totally new product or maybe your business is an unusual combination of many different activities. In this scenario, try to locate a set of benchmarks for a business type that's at least similar to yours in some way or other.

TIP

If you've already been trading for a couple of years or more, you can also benchmark your financial projections against Profit & Loss reports from your own business for previous years. For example, if results from previous years show that your wages usually average 30 percent of sales, but your Profit & Loss Projection for next year shows that wages only equal 25 percent of sales, you have probably made an error in your projections.

	A	B	C	D
1		My Business	Expenses as % of Sales	Benchmark Expenses % of Sales
2	Total Sales	$ 285,000.00		
3				
4	Drugs, supplies, consumables	$ 9,300.00	3.3%	2.2%
5	Wages and salaries	$ 93,000.00	32.6%	25.3%
6	Staff oncosts	$ 13,950.00	4.9%	2.2%
7	Rent of premises	$ 18,200.00	6.4%	5.5%
8	Depreciation/lease/hire purchase	$ 12,200.00	4.3%	2.7%
9	All other expenses	$ 22,050.00	7.7%	13.1%
10	Total Expenses	$ 168,700.00		
11				
12	Net Profit	$ 116,300.00	40.8%	49.2%

FIGURE 10-2: Looking at expense percentages is part of the benchmarking process.

Keeping the Wolf from the Door

If you're starting a new business and you have very little savings or start-up capital, you may find you have very little to live on while building up your business. In this scenario, I can't stress enough how important it is to create a budget not only for business expenses, but also for personal expenses.

Even if your business is already up and running, creating a budget for personal expenses is usually still a good idea. You must ensure that your business is going to generate enough income to cover your personal expenses. If not, you may need to make changes to your business plan (such as adjusting expenses or increasing income) or, alternatively, make some changes to your personal spending patterns.

Your budget for personal expenses works in much the same way as your budget for business expenses, except that the kinds of expenses in your private life are very different. You can find a heap of free personal budgeting apps for use on your smartphone. Unless you already have a personal budgeting system in place, I suggest you download one of these apps and use it as a prompt to analyze how much you currently spend on what, and how much you need each week to survive.

TIP

If your personal expenses look as if they're likely to exceed the profit your business generates, and you don't have any other source of income or savings, one of your options is to see if you can cut back on your personal expenses. You may be surprised to find how cheaply you can live if you really have to. Your flexibility depends on your stage of life — announcing that you're about to start a business as a street performer two weeks before your partner is due to give birth to twins is never going to go down well — but, mostly, you'll be surprised how you can simplify even the most complicated of lives.

REMEMBER

Sometimes a business can survive, but leave a broken relationship in its wake. One reason business plans are so important is that they can help you to understand the risks involved not just on a financial level, but on a personal level also.

And on that cheery note, this chapter comes to a close.

Chapter **11**
Assembling Your First Financial Forecast

I n this chapter, I pull together all the information that goes into the financial forecast known as your Profit & Loss Projection, including pricing and sales projections, costs and gross profit projections, and expense projections. This helps you arrive at an estimate of just how much profit your business is likely to generate over the next 12 months.

Looking at your likely profits can be an emotional turning point when creating a business plan, especially if this is the first Profit & Loss Projection you've ever made. Few of us go into business without wanting to make a profit and, if the Profit & Loss Projection shows limited profits for what's likely to be a heap of work, you'll probably feel rather discouraged.

Feeling discouraged is okay. If your business model is a dud, you're better to quit now while you're still ahead than spend another year or two on an idea that will never fly. On the other hand, if you suspect that your essential idea is still strong, this part of the planning process gives you another chance to look at all your figures and experiment with pricing, costs, and expenses.

Of course, you may find that your financial projections predict a business with a rosy future. That's great. Nothing is better than a promising business plan. However, in the last part of this chapter, I spend a bit of time explaining how you can use AI to perform scenario analysis. What if sales were 10 percent less, or expenses 10 percent more? AI is an incredibly efficient way to assess how robust your plan is, and the likely risks involved.

Building Your Profit & Loss Projection

So you're ready to create your first Profit & Loss Projection for the next 12 months? Then make yourself a hot cup of something and get ready to see how all the bits of your plan fit together.

Step one: Projected sales

The top of any Profit & Loss Projection always starts by showing income, then cost of sales, then gross profit. I talk about calculating gross profit in detail in Chapter 9, so if you haven't already worked through your gross profit projections, scoot over to Chapter 9 first. With these workings in place, you're ready to go.

Here's how to add sales to your Profit & Loss Projection:

1. **Using Excel (or any other spreadsheet software), open up your Gross Profit Projection worksheet.**

   Refer to Chapter 9 for more about this worksheet. The idea is that you've already created a worksheet estimating both your sales and your cost of sales for the next 12 months.

   Note: If your sales projections are very simple and you don't have any cost of sales, you may not need to create a Gross Profit Projection. In this case, you can simply start with a Profit and Loss Projection and enter your sales estimates from scratch.

2. **Rest your mouse on the tab at the bottom of this worksheet that says Sheet1 and right-click.**

   Or, if you're using a Macintosh, hold down the control button and then click with your mouse.

3. **Click Rename and then type GrossProfit as the name.**

4. Rest your mouse on the tab that says Sheet2 and right-click.

5. Rename this tab to become ProfitLoss.

You have now created and named two separate worksheets within a workbook. The first worksheet is called GrossProfit and the second worksheet is called ProfitLoss.

6. On the ProfitLoss worksheet, label the months along the top (in row 1).

7. Go to your GrossProfit tab, and highlight the row where you recorded the grand total for sales each month. Right-click with your mouse (or control then click if you're on a Mac) and select Copy.

8. Return to the ProfitLoss tab and click on cell B2.

Cell B2 is where the first month of total sales is going to show.

9. Right-click (or control then click for Mac users) and select Paste Special.

10. Click the Paste Link button that appears in the bottom-left of this dialogue box.

Before your eyes, the sales for each month should appear right across row 2, similar to Figure 11-1. (I just show the first few months here, but you get the general idea.)

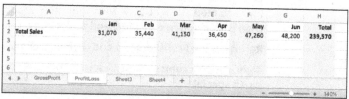

	A	B	C	D	E	F	G	H
1		Jan	Feb	Mar	Apr	May	Jun	Total
2	Total Sales	31,070	35,440	41,150	36,450	47,260	48,200	239,570
3								
4								
5								
6								

GrossProfit ProfitLoss Sheet3 Sheet4 +

FIGURE 11-1: Total sales form the first line of your Profit & Loss Projection.

TIP

Are you wondering why I've gone to all the trouble of creating multiple worksheets and linking one sheet to another, rather than just copying and pasting the estimated total sales? The reason I suggest you work in this way is so your total sales will update automatically whenever you tweak your detailed sales. For example, maybe I want to see what would happen if I lift my pricing by 10 percent. All I have to do is tweak the pricing in my Sales Projection worksheet and this flows automatically through to my Profit & Loss Projection.

Of course, if you're a very small business and you don't want to go to the trouble of splitting up your income in any kind of detail — you just want to type in an estimated dollar total for each month — then you don't need to bother creating a separate worksheet for sales projections.

Step two: Variable costs

If your business has no variable costs, you can skip this step entirely. However, if your business has variable costs (and refer to Chapter 9 if you're not sure whether this is the case), then the next stage is to bring these figures across.

Again, you need to have your gross profit projections complete before you do this step. If you haven't, you may need to have a quick look through the last few pages of Chapter 9 before you continue.

1. **Open up your Gross Profit Projection worksheet.**

   I'm following on from the instructions in the previous section of this chapter ('Step one: Insert your projected sales forecasts') and I'm assuming you've already inserted a row showing projected sales.

2. **Go to the GrossProfit tab, and highlight the rows where you recorded the total for cost of sales and gross profit for each month. Right-click with your mouse (or control then click if you're on a Mac) and select Copy.**

3. **Return to the ProfitLoss tab and click on cell A4.**

4. **Right-click (or control then click for Mac users) and select Paste Special.**

5. **Click the Paste Link button that appears in the bottom-left of this dialogue box.**

   Your total cost of sales for each month, as well as Gross Profit, should now appear below your sales. (If a bunch of zeros appear in row 5, which may happen because row 5 is blank in the Gross Profit worksheet, simply delete these zeros.)

6. Format the cells if necessary.

Sometimes the formatting doesn't come across when you link one worksheet to another. So feel free to add bold to your headings and format the amounts to include dollar signs.

7. Check your results.

By the time you're done, your worksheet should look similar to Figure 11-2, showing total sales, cost of sales and gross profit for the next 12 months. This worksheet has exactly the same figures as your gross profit projection, but with the difference that it displays much less detail. This less detailed format is what many investors or bank managers would expect to see as an overall financial projection.

	A	B	C	D	E	F	G	H
1		Jan	Feb	Mar	Apr	May	Jun	Total
2	Total Sales	31,070	35,440	41,150	36,450	47,260	48,200	239,570
3								
4	Total Cost of Sales	12,428	14,176	16,460	14,580	18,904	19,280	95,828
5								
6	Gross Profit	18,642	21,264	24,690	21,870	28,356	28,920	143,742
7								

GrossProfit ProfitLoss Sheet3 Sheet4 +

− ▬▬▬▬ ● ▬▬▬ + 140%

FIGURE 11-2: Cost of sales and gross profit show below total sales on your Profit & Loss Projection.

Step three: Expenses budget

Step three in building your Profit & Loss Projection is to add detail regarding your expenses. Chapter 10 explains how to create a worksheet that accurately forecasts business expenses on a monthly basis, and I'm going to assume here that you've already completed this worksheet.

Here's how to add expenses to your Profit & Loss Projection:

1. Open up your expenses worksheet.

Refer to Chapter 10 for details on how to create this spreadsheet.

2. Highlight every single cell that has anything in it.

In other words, click in the top-left cell and drag your mouse down to the bottom-right cell.

3. Right-click and select Copy.

Or press the command button and then click if you're a sensible Macintosh person.

4. Go to your Profit & Loss Projection workbook and click the ProfitLoss tab.

5. Click cell A8 in this worksheet, then right-click and select Paste.

What I'm meaning here is you click in the first column below the Gross Profit totals. When you click Paste, you're copying everything from your expenses worksheet into your Profit & Loss worksheet.

6. At the bottom of the expenses, insert a row called Total Expenses. Add a Sum formula so that Total Expenses automatically calculates the expenses listed above.

Figure 11-3 shows what this will look like. You now have a Profit & Loss worksheet that starts with sales, then shows cost of sales and gross profit, and finally lists all your expenses.

TIP

Are you wondering why I suggest you copy across all the expense totals from your worksheet, rather than just a single total for expenses in the same way as you did for sales and cost of sales? The reason is partly historical. Accountants, business advisors and investors are accustomed to a standard format for Profit & Loss projections, and this format typically provides a summary of sales and cost of sales, and more detail for expenses.

7. Add a line for Net Profit at the bottom of your worksheet, inserting a formula that subtracts Total Expenses from Gross Profit.

In Figure 11-3, the formula for January's net profit would be =B6-B27. Your formula will be different because you're bound to have a different number of rows for your expenses, but I'm sure you get the general idea.

Notice that in Figure 11-3, I also added a final column showing the total for each row, so that I can see the total sales, gross profit, expenses, and net profit for the whole period combined.

	A	B	C	D	E	F	G	H	I
1		Jan	Feb	Mar	Apr	May	Jun	Total	
2	Total Sales	31,070	35,440	41,150	36,450	47,260	48,200	239,570	
3									
4	Total Cost of Sales	12,428	14,176	16,460	14,580	18,904	19,280	95,828	
5									
6	Gross Profit	18,642	21,264	24,690	21,870	28,356	28,920	143,742	
7									
8	Accounting Fees	-	2,000	-	-	-	-		
9	Bank Charges	100	100	100	100	100	100	600	
10	Communication Expenses	380	380	380	380	380	380	2,280	
11	Consultant Expenses	300	300	300	300	300	300	1,800	
12	Insurance	280	280	280	280	280	280	1,680	
13	Interest Expense	520	520	520	520	520	520	3,120	
14	IT Expenses	450	450	450	450	450	450	2,700	
15	Lease Expenses	800	800	800	800	800	800	4,800	
16	Marketing Expenses	1,200	1,200	1,200	1,200	1,200	1,200	7,200	
17	Merchant Fees	621	709	823	729	945	964	4,791	
18	Motor Vehicle Expenses	350	350	350	350	1,800	350	3,550	
19	Office Supplies	150	150	150	150	150	150	900	
20	Rental Expense	3,250	3,250	3,250	3,250	3,250	3,250	19,500	
21	Repairs and Maintenance	500	500	500	500	500	500	3,000	
22	Staff Amenities	300	300	300	300	300	300	1,800	
23	Travel Expenses	350	350	350	350	350	350	2,100	
24	Utilities	600	-	-	600	-	-		
25	Wages and Salaries	3,600	3,600	4,500	3,600	3,600	4,500	23,400	
26	Wages oncosts	540	540	675	540	540	675	3,510	
27	Total Expenses	14,291	15,779	14,928	14,399	15,465	15,069	89,931	
28									
29	Net Profit	4,351	5,485	9,762	7,471	12,891	13,851	53,811	
30									
31									

GrossProfit ProfitLoss Sheet3 Sheet4 +

140%

FIGURE 11-3: Your completed Profit & Loss Projection.

Step four: Think about tax

If you're a sole trader or partnership, the amount of personal tax you pay depends on many factors, including whether you have any other sources of income other than the business. For this reason, I suggest that you don't include personal income tax as an expense on your Profit & Loss Projection, but that you make an allowance for tax when calculating how much you require in personal drawings. (See 'Assessing whether your net profit is reasonable, or not' later in this chapter for more info.)

However, if your business has a company structure, you need to include company tax as an expense on your Profit & Loss Projection based on the profits you make. To do this, simply add a final line to your Profit & Loss report called Company Tax Expense. Calculate this expense at the correct percentage of company tax and then add a final line to your worksheet called Net Profit After Tax.

Step five: Check your sums

You're not quite done yet. The last step is to check that you got everything right. (Spreadsheets are great in the way they calculate everything for you, but get one formula wrong, and the error can spread like a dropped stitch on a knitting project.)

So here's your checklist:

REMEMBER

>> Save your workings and then make a copy of your Gross Profit Projection worksheet. On the copy, change your prices to $10 for every product, change your unit costs to $1, and change the unit sales to 100 units per month. Check that your gross profit comes out at $900 every month.

>> Grab a calculator and manually check the sums for the first and the last month in your forecast. Check total sales, gross profit, total expenses, and net profit.

>> If your business is already up and running, review your Profit & Loss report for the most recent month. Plug in the figures from this report into the first month of your Profit & Loss Projection and check that the net profit in your projection matches with the report.

All good? Then you're ready to move onto the next part of your business plan, which is where you get to ponder whether the forecasted profit is what you need it to be . . .

Analyzing Net Profit

As I mention in the preceding section, one of the primary purposes of your Profit & Loss Projection is to figure out how much profit you'll be left with at the end of the day. This result enables you to decide whether you want to continue with this business, whether you need to change your business model in some way, and whether you're making a reasonable rate of return on your investment.

Calculating net profit margins

So, to do a quick recap:

- » Gross profit equals sales less variable costs.
- » Net profit equals gross profit less fixed expenses.
- » Gross profit is always more than net profit.
- » The more you sell, the more gross profit you make.
- » The more you sell, the more net profit you make.

To calculate your net profit margin, you first calculate your net profit, and then you divide this amount by the value of total sales and multiply the result by 100. For example, if my sales are $200,000 a year and my net profit is $6,000, my net profit margin is 3 percent (that's $6,000 divided by $200,000 multiplied by 100).

Assessing whether your net profit is reasonable, or not

A specific percentage rate at which you can say that a net profit margin is reasonable doesn't exist, because too many variables affect this judgment. However, you should be able to establish for yourself a rate that you think is reasonable, and run with that.

The biggest factor to take into account is whether the net profit on your Profit & Loss Projection includes payment for your time. If your business has a sole trader or partnership structure, the final net profit on your Profit & Loss Projection represents the profit that your business generates before you see a single cent in payment for your time. Therefore, the net profits (and hence the net profit margins) need to be much higher than for an equivalent business with a company structure. (In contrast, if your business has a company structure, you need to include your monthly wages as part of your expenses, and so payment for your time is already accounted for.)

Another approach is to think about how much you need to live comfortably. If the net profit of your business is more than what you require to live (or, if you're a company, the net profit plus your wages), this figure is probably reasonable. However, if the net profit doesn't cover your personal expenses, your business has a problem.

TIP

When looking at your projected net profit, I recommend that you look at the margin for error. If your Profit & Loss Projection shows a high level of sales and a similarly high level of expenses, with only a narrow net profit margin left at the end of the day, you must ask yourself whether you have enough room for error. (I talk about this topic later in this chapter, in 'Using AI to assess the risk involved'.) For example, if a reduction of only 10 percent in sales could mean you can't pay your rent or make your mortgage repayments, this net profit is probably not quite enough.

Thinking ahead further ahead

In this chapter (and most other chapters in this book) I suggest you work on financial projections for the next 12-month period only. I make this suggestion for two reasons: First, if you're just getting started in business, trying to make financial projections for two, three, or even five years into the future can quickly feel like a make-believe exercise, because so much about what lies ahead is unknown. Second, what I'm trying to do in this book is to get you to create financial projections yourself, and I don't want to discourage you by making things any trickier than they need to be.

However, if you only do financial projections for 12 months into the future, you may not get a true picture of what lies ahead, particularly if you have strong growth patterns or your business is just getting started. Sometimes, you need to extend your forecasts for 24 or even 36 months ahead in order to predict at what point your business will really start to flourish and generate decent profits.

Extending your Profit & Loss Projection is easy — simply copy and paste the results from the 12th month across to additional columns, and then change the figures as need be. All the same principles apply — you're simply extending the forecast for another year or two.

Taking Things a Step Further

A Profit & Loss Projection for the next 12 months provides a bare minimum for the financial part of your business plan. Other financial reports you may wish to include are a scenario analysis worksheet and a Cashflow Projection.

Using AI to assess the risk involved

If you're doing a plan for a new business or a business that's currently undergoing significant change, one of the major challenges is how unknown everything is. For example, maybe you're planning to open up a new retail outlet, a dentistry practice, or a health spa. When it comes to forecasting your sales, you may feel that you're just plucking figures out of the air.

Figure-plucking (a highly technical term that I'm particularly fond of) is a dangerous thing. In an attempt to discourage this process, in Chapter 8 I focus on planning for sales in detail, analyzing the number of items or services you have to sell in order to reach projected monthly sales totals. In Chapter 10, I also talk about benchmarking, and explain how important it is to research industry averages. (I suggest talking to your accountant, looking up benchmarking services, using AI apps, or contacting industry associations.) However, even with all this solid groundwork in place, you may still be wondering about the accuracy of your financial projections.

In this situation, I recommend you do a bit of scenario analysis, varying your income, cost of sales and expenses upwards or downwards by 10 or 20 percent to see what happens. Playing with percentages in this way is a good method for assessing how robust your plans are, and how much wriggle room you have to play with.

TIP

The most thorough way to complete your scenario analysis is to make a copy of your financial projections and modify the figures. However, this process can be quite time-consuming, and a quicker approach is to use AI to help.

The exact requests you need to use will vary, depending on your AI app; however, for example, at the time of writing, I was able to go to ChatGPT and type in the following question: 'Can you look at a financial forecast and see what would happen if sales decreased by 5%?'

I was prompted to copy and paste my spreadsheet results and, once complete, ChatGPT provided the answer. Next, I asked, 'What if sales decreased by 5%, my gross profit margin decreased by 5%, and my expenses increased by 8%?' In a few seconds, I was able to see what financial impact these variations would have on my bottom line.

While perhaps chilling in the accuracy and speed of its results, this particular use of AI is undeniably efficient.

Looking at cashflow

Did you know that your business can make a profit yet can run out of cash? Of all the perils of business, one of the most disheartening has to be a promising enterprise that grows so fast that it starves itself of funds. However, if you have an eye to the future, not to mention the ability to create a Cashflow Projection report, you should be able to predict when a cash crunch is going to occur. You can then plan accordingly, maybe approaching the bank for additional finance, timing expenses differently, or consciously slowing growth.

A Cashflow Projection is very similar to a Profit & Loss Projection, but with a few notable differences. I summarize these differences in Table 11-1.

TABLE 11-1 Differences between a Profit & Loss Projection and a Cashflow Projection

A Profit & Loss Projection . . .	A Cashflow Projection . . .
Shows sales in the month that they're made	Provides additional detail to show sales in the month that payment is received
Doesn't include incoming funds from loans or other sources of finance	Includes additional detail showing all sources of funds, including loans and capital contributions
Doesn't include consumer taxes (GST, VAT, or sales tax) but shows all figures net of tax	More complex Cashflow Projections may show figures including tax, and then show tax payments separately
Shows only the interest on loan repayments, not the full value of the loan repayments	Shows the full value of loan repayments
Shows cost of sales (the cost of materials and so on) at the time a sale is made, regardless of when materials were purchased	Provides additional detail to show the purchase of materials in the month payment is made
Doesn't include capital expenditure or start-up costs	Includes all cash outflows, including capital expenditure and start-up costs

A Profit & Loss Projection . . .	A Cashflow Projection . . .
Doesn't include owner drawings (relevant for sole traders and partnerships only)	May include owner drawings (relevant for sole traders and partnerships only)
Includes no information regarding likely cash available	Forecasts the closing bank balance for the end of each month

Is a Cashflow Projection an essential part of your business plan? If any of the following apply to your business, and where the rate of growth is putting pressure on cashflow, the answer is probably 'yes':

» You offer credit to customers and your sales go up and down from month to month.

» You hold inventory and inventory levels vary from month to month, or are likely to increase as your business grows.

» You have major start-up costs or purchases of capital equipment that aren't shown in your Profit & Loss Projection.

» Your loan repayments are significantly different to interest expense (although an alternative approach is simply to show the full value of loan repayments in your Profit & Loss Projection).

Chapter **12**

Perfecting the Final Pitch

People have a fundamental need to listen to stories — whether these stories be a yarn told around the fireside, a block-buster novel, a TikTok video, or a heartfelt story about a journey as yet unfinished.

For this reason, the best business plans are ones that tell a story. This might be a story about you, about your business, or perhaps about how your idea has the potential to change lives.

If you've been working on your plan over the course of many weeks, you may have ended up with a ragtag assembly of hand-written notes, Word files, financial projections and reports. In this chapter, I look at how you fit these pieces together to assemble not just a sensible justification for your business, but also a story that can inspire yourself and others.

Exploring Different Formats

Who is going to read your plan? Are you writing a business plan for your eyes only, aiming to provide structure for your business model? Or are you writing this plan hoping to persuade a loans manager or investor to lend to, or invest in, your business?

The best way to present your plan depends on the intended audience. In the first part of this chapter, I look at what's involved in creating a pitch deck, a quick one-page plan, or a full business plan.

Preparing for your *Shark Tank* moment

Have you ever watched *Shark Tank*, the TV show where entrepreneurs pitch their idea in three minutes to a group of hard-nosed investors? (If you haven't, I suggest you take a few minutes to watch some shorts on YouTube.) *Shark Tank* participants are required to deliver a pitch in just a few minutes, using both public speaking skills and something called a *pitch deck*.

A pitch deck is a slideshow, typically using 10 to 20 slides, that aims to tell the story of an opportunity or business idea. Strong visual elements are key to a good pitch deck, delivering maximum impact with minimal text.

You won't find a right or wrong way to create a pitch deck, but the common convention is to start by explaining the problem that your business model will solve. The slideshow then proceeds to explain the proposed solution, followed by slides that touch on market size, business models, your team, and the competition. (The preceding chapters in this book enable you to do most of the foundational work for creating slides addressing these topics.) Finally, a pitch deck concludes with the 'ask' of how much investment you're seeking. (See 'Popping the question', later in this chapter, for more about this topic.)

In short, a pitch deck skips the high level of detail typically found in a business plan, and instead is designed to tell a story that captivates the interest of potential investors, and so pave the way for future conversations.

If you're not pitching to investors, you probably don't need a pitch deck. Nonetheless, an hour or two spent online looking at pitch decks that others have created for business ventures similar to yours may well be productive in sparking a more entrepreneurial mindset, or for generating more ideas in how you can sell your business.

Keeping things to a single page

Different from a pitch deck, and a world apart from a full business plan, is a one-page business plan. A one-page plan isn't a slide show, and nor is it a pitch; rather, it is a summary of your business idea. Typically, a one-page plan details the problem your product or service will solve and why this represents a good opportunity, followed by short descriptions of your industry, target market, marketing plan, financial model and how much funding you're looking for. A one-page plan also sets out what it is that your business will do differently from others. (For more on this, check out Chapter 2.)

One-page plans can be handy if you're time poor and still sketching out your business idea; the discipline of distilling everything into a single page is excellent for bringing clarity to your thinking. However, a one-page plan doesn't replace a full business plan, and incurs the risk that you skate over necessary detail, such as the analysis of competitors and industry trends, or the creation of detailed financial projections.

In short, if you're still developing your business idea and seeking a format that summarizes your initial thoughts, a one-page plan may serve you well. However, as I talk about in the previous section, if you're thinking of using a one-page plan to pitch to an investor, you're probably best with a pitch deck instead. Finally, if you're hoping that a one-page plan will be more efficient than a full plan, do be aware that there is no such thing as a free lunch — this absence of detail may cost you dearly!

Structuring a full plan

Assuming you don't want to create a pitch deck or a quick one-page summary (refer to the preceding two sections for details), how do you go about assembling a full business plan? A format that works well (and which mirrors how I've organized the chapters in this book) is as follows:

- **A cover page and table of contents:** Your final business plan will probably end up being between 15 and 20 pages long, so a table of contents helps you and others find what's what. If you plan to share this plan with others outside of your company, you may also choose to include a non-disclosure agreement at the front.

- **An Executive Summary:** See 'Crafting an eloquent summary', later in this chapter, for details of what this should include.

- **Your point of difference and strategic advantage:** In the ideal world, you cover these topics in your Executive Summary. For more on these topics, refer to Chapters 2 and 3.

- **Where you see you and your business in the future:** I devote a whole chapter to the topic of separating yourself from your business and 'thinking big' in Chapter 4. However, for the purpose of your plan, you can distil the vision you have for growth into a sentence of two. This may form part of your Executive Summary, or could be part of your ask for funding.

- **A summary of strengths and weaknesses, opportunities or threats:** I cover SWOT analysis in Chapter 5.

- **A competitor analysis:** Chapters 3 and 6 talk about competitor analysis and competitive strategy. Providing a summary of this analysis in your business plan demonstrates to outside readers that you've done your homework.

- **A marketing plan:** Chapter 6 provides a complete summary of how to construct a marketing plan. You don't include the whole marketing plan in your business plan, but you should include a summary of your target market, sales targets, marketing strategies, customer service plan, and marketing activities.

- **A people plan:** See 'Covering All Bases', later in this chapter, for details.

- **A summary of operations, if appropriate:** See 'Covering All Bases', later in this chapter, for details.

>> **A risk-management plan, if appropriate:** Are you setting up business as a tree-lopper, circus acrobat, security consultant, or cryptocurrency trader? The more risk in your business, the more important it is to include a risk-management strategy in your plan, with a risk matrix being the most commonly accepted model for presenting this information.

>> **Financial reports:** See 'Showing Where the Money's At', later in this chapter, for details.

>> **The ask:** Ah, the gentle art of asking for money. I cover this delicate topic later in this chapter, in 'Popping the question'.

>> **An appendix:** Super-detailed information such as résumés of the management team, product photos, legal agreements, or market research is often best provided as an online link. If providing info in this way isn't practical, including an appendix at the end of your plan can work just as well.

Don't feel obliged to stick to this suggested structure. In particular, if you've chosen to use business planning software (see 'Using AI for What It's Good At', later in this chapter), you'll almost certainly end up with a structure that's slightly different. The important thing is that you cover these topics in a way that makes sense both to you and to your likely readers.

Building a Cohesive Narrative

A business plan has many different sections, and one of the challenges can be finding a common thread that weaves its way from the first page to the last. Examples of what this thread could be include the following:

>> An imperative to act on an opportunity very quickly

>> A problem/solution narrative, such as the problem you're solving and why you're best placed to deliver

>> A significant profit potential, if only investment can be secured

While writing your plan, try to weave this thread through as a connecting message that binds the different sections of your plan together. In addition, keep returning to the question of what you want readers to feel. How can you best convey a feeling of inspiration or perhaps even excitement, and make others confident in your ability to deliver?

Telling a story that changes minds

As I've alluded to a few times so far in this chapter, the best business plans are ones that tell a story.

One approach is to tell the story of how your business product or service will, or has already, affected the lives of others. So, if you're starting a business consulting about permaculture, spend time talking about the transformation permaculture practice can have on the land and its ecology; if you're providing a service to people with disability, share how you improve the lives of those you work with; if you're setting up a manufacturing business in a regional town, describe the impact on community that new jobs can deliver.

An alternative approach, especially if you feel your business doesn't lend itself to inspirational stories, might be to tell your own story. Perhaps you're a single parent with three kids, and your business represents a ticket to financial independence; perhaps you left school at 14 but have taught yourself the skills necessary to start your own venture; perhaps you have already achieved some extraordinary things in your life, but this business represents a pivotal moment for you.

REMEMBER

Stories don't have to be on a grand scale to capture the imaginations of others, but can be relatively simple, especially if you can manage to convey your own love and excitement for what it is that you do.

Crafting an eloquent summary

Most business plans start with what's called an Executive Summary, a couple of pages that encapsulate everything that's about to follow. Seemingly straightforward, this summary can be agonizingly tricky to write, as you aim to provide enough detail to inspire the reader while remaining brilliantly concise.

TIP

You may even find it easiest to delay writing your Executive Summary until after you've worked on the rest of your plan, so that you can gain more clarity as to how the different elements fit together.

Here are some pointers for what makes for a strong Executive Summary:

>> **The context:** A description of your business and its products or services, or of your business idea.

>> **What drives you:** More traditionally referred to as a mission statement, here's where you get to say something a bit more aspirational about why you're in business and what you hope to achieve.

>> **The problem you want to solve:** If your business isn't trading yet, and you're selling a new idea or concept, leap straight into describing the problem you're trying to solve, and why this presents an opportunity. You want to convince readers that your idea is unique and valuable, and has the potential to succeed.

>> **What's different about you, and your strategic advantage:** Even if you're proposing to start a business that others have done before you (anything from gardening to physio, from consulting to events management), you still want to explain what you're going to do better than others. (For more about identifying strategic advantage and differentiating yourself from competitors, refer to Chapter 2.)

>> **A compelling story:** If possible, try to tell a story that will inspire readers to keep reading. This could be a story about how you had the idea to start this business, or a narrative about yourself and any special skills or talents that you have. Alternatively, this story could be about the scope of the opportunity.

>> **Your industry, the competition, and where the opportunities lie:** Talk about your particular industry, what the trends are, and where you see the opportunities. (Chapters 3 and 5 help you with compiling this info.)

>> **You and your crew:** Describe the structure of your business, who the owners are, who the employees are and, if possible, what makes your team a cut above.

>> **High-level financials:** I'm not talking detailed projections here, but rather two or three sentences that include the value of projected sales, gross profit and net profit for next 12 months, as well as the rate of expected growth.

>> **The ask:** If part of the purpose of this business plan is to persuade an investor or lender to give you money, include how much it is you're looking for and how you intend to use this investment. I suggest you provide more detail about this request later in the plan (see 'Popping the question', later in this chapter) but the benefit of summarizing the ask at the outset is that it sets the context, allowing the reader to focus on what you intend to achieve with the funding.

TIP

If you're in doubt about what to omit and what to include in your Executive Summary, keep in mind that nobody reading your plan from start to finish should stumble across a crucial piece of information deep inside the plan itself.

Presenting the context

In Chapter 5, I talk about minimizing risk and maximizing profitability by staying ahead of trends, and I explain how to draw up a SWOT analysis to identify your strengths, weaknesses, opportunities and threats.

Take the time to return to the work you did, and reflect on whether you need to edit your SWOT analysis to fit more closely in the overall context of your plan. Specifically, take time to check the following:

>> If your plan includes a risk matrix, does this matrix address any weaknesses identified in your SWOT analysis?

>> If your SWOT analysis identified positive industry trends, does your business model and/or marketing plan capitalize on these?

>> Is the competitive or strategic advantage that you articulate in your Executive Summary reflected in the opportunities and strengths of your SWOT analysis?

>> Is your SWOT analysis framed to highlight the overriding opportunity that your business plan identifies?

At risk of stating the obvious, the idea is to demonstrate to readers of your plan that not only have you considered the outside world and how it may impact your business, but also your response to these trends is integral to your business strategy.

Covering All Bases

Depending on the scale of your existing or proposed business, other elements you should consider including in your plan are a description of your team, an overview of operations, and a summary of your goals.

When talking about your team, a concise description of the key people in your business, along with who is responsible for doing what, will usually suffice. Include a short description of each person's role, relevant work experience and qualifications, as well as the unique skills that each person contributes, taking care that your description of people's skills resonates with the SWOT analysis in your plan. If you're only just getting started — maybe you don't have any employees yet — include details of people in your network who are assisting you, such as your accountant, business mentor, or family and friends.

If you're a manufacturer or wholesaler, I suggest you include a brief summary of operations management at some point in your plan. For manufacturers, this summary typically describes the process of manufacture, where and how your product is manufactured, and what mechanisms you have in place for order fulfilment and delivery. For wholesalers, this summary describes automations, order fulfilment systems and delivery logistics.

REMEMBER

As part of your description of operations for your business, return to the question of strategic advantage (a topic explored in Chapters 2 and 3). Is an aspect of operations integral to your strategic advantage, such as a highly competitive or innovative way of manufacturing or distributing products? If so, take the time to describe how your unique location, skill set, software systems or distribution networks influence operations, and how they serve to provide your business with the potential for a higher rate of return than your competitors.

Finally, as you pull the elements of your plan together, start listing your goals, and the necessary actions you need to take, remembering that the ideal goal is a SMART one: Specific, Measurable, Achievable, Realistic and Time-bound. A table sorted by date that lists goals and/or milestones, detailing what needs to happen by when, can be an excellent addition to a business plan, demonstrating a certain pragmatism and organizational ability.

Showing Where the Money's At

In working on the financial part of your plan, you may well have ended up with a wide selection of documents — everything from product costings to price comparisons, from historical sales reports to budgets for the years ahead. Which reports should you include in your final plan, and in what sequence should you present these?

The next couple of sections explain what you might include in this section of your plan, and also how to broach that most delicate of requests — namely, how much money you're looking for, and why.

Deciding what financial reports to include

Which financial reports to include in a plan depends on the stage a business is at, and the complexity of its finances. For businesses that haven't started trading yet, I suggest the following:

>> **A summary of start-up expenses:** I talk about start-up expenses in Chapter 7.

>> **Sales and gross profit projections for the next 12 months:** Chapters 8 and 9 explain how to assemble these reports.

>> **A Profit & Loss Projection for the next 12 months:** Chapters 10 and 11 explain what to do here.

>> **Break-even analysis:** I don't have scope in this book to cover how to calculate your break-even analysis, but you can easily find a template online.

For businesses that are already trading, financial reports should include:

>> **A Profit & Loss report for the last 12 months:** If the figures for the past 12 months are unusual for any reason, include some notes as to why.

>> **A Balance Sheet for the date that your Profit & Loss report goes up to:** So, if your Profit & Loss report goes for the 12 months from April to March, generate a Balance Sheet for March 31.

>> **A Profit & Loss Projection for the next 12 months:** If your business is growing quickly, extend this projection and include figures for the next 24 to 36 months as well. (For subsequent years, you can summarize projections to include one column per quarter, rather than one column per month.)

If your business is already trading, but the rate of growth is putting pressure on cashflow, you should include all of the preceding financial reports as well as a Cashflow Projection and a Balance Sheet Projection for the end of this Cashflow period. You're best to subscribe to a business planning app in order to compile these rather technical reports.

REMEMBER

As you pull together the different elements of your plan, pay attention to consistency. For example, if your marketing plan shows significant growth, is this growth reflected in your people plan, and in your Profit & Loss projection? Similarly, if your SWOT analysis shows a weakness in working with social media, and social media is foundational to your marketing plan, does your budget allow for paying for social media advice?

Selling scalability

For many businesses, perhaps even the majority of businesses, the amount of profit you make is dependent on scale. When a business model is highly scalable, you have the potential to increase revenue significantly without a proportionate increase in expenses, often leveraging automations or technology to do so. For example, software applications are a highly scalable business: Once developed, software can usually be sold to an unlimited number of customers with minimal additional costs or physical infrastructure.

For investors, scalability is everything. If you know that doubling your revenue will quadruple your profit, take the time to include Profit & Loss Projections that prove this to be the case. These projections may be the clincher for securing additional investment.

TIP

Use AI apps such as ChatGPT to explore the scalability of your business model. Upload your existing financial reports (taking care to remove any identifying or personal information first, of course) and from there ask questions such as 'If income were to increase by 50 percent and expenses increased by only 20 percent, what would my profit be?'

Popping the question

Earlier in this chapter, in the section 'Crafting an eloquent summary', I suggest that you include any requests for finance in your Executive Summary. This request might go something like, 'We are seeking a business loan for $50,000 to allow us to expand into new premises. The funds will be spent on fit-out, rent in advance and marketing'.

This summary sets the context for anybody reading the plan, and the financials section of your plan then fleshes out this request in more detail. How best to frame this request depends on whether you're pitching to an investor, or to a bank.

Seeking a loan from a bank

In general, banks are interested in strong profitability, what collateral you can offer against the loan, your ability to service repayments, the stability of your business, the accuracy of your financial reports, and your personal credit rating. They'll also want to know exactly what you intend to use the finance for.

TIP

Use an online loan calculator tool to figure out the interest you should expect to pay on the loan amount you're requesting, as well as the likely repayment schedule. Don't forget to include the anticipated loan interest as an expense in your Profit & Loss Projection, and also include the full value of proposed loan repayments in your Cashflow Projection. (Alternatively, if your plan doesn't include a Cashflow Projection, show the full value of the loan repayment in the Profit & Loss Projection.)

If you require this loan for working capital, perhaps because your business is growing or you have particular times of the year when cash is particularly tight, a Cashflow Projection is ideal for corroborating your need for additional finance.

Pitching to investors

Typically, investors are on the hunt for a clever business idea that offers the potential to yield above-average returns. In contrast to banks, investors are less interested in past profitability and stability, and are more interested in future profitability and the potential for rapid growth. They may also be interested in leveraging their own expertise to facilitate this growth.

Similar to asking a bank for a loan, be explicit about how much funding you're seeking, and how you intend to use these funds. However, in addition, include a description of the impact this funding will have, including before and after Profit & Loss Projections demonstrating this likely impact. As I mention in 'Selling scalability', earlier in this chapter, demonstrating scalability, if you can, is key.

Any investment in somebody else's business represents a risk, and investors are generally more willing to take risks if they see the potential for high returns. As part of your ask, include the potential ROI (return on investment) for the investor, and clarify whether you're asking for a loan or selling a stake in your business. If asking for a loan, what interest rate are you proposing to pay, and what is the proposed term of the loan? If selling a stake in your business, what percentage of equity are you offering, what will be the likely rate of return, and how do you propose profits will be distributed?

REMEMBER

Regardless of whether you're asking for a loan or selling equity, make sure you outline potential exit strategies also. How will the investor get their money out, and when?

Using AI for What It's Good At

Creating business plans is one of the things that AI does pretty well. By AI, I'm not really talking about ChatGPT or an equivalent (although these apps can undoubtedly help), but rather a business planning software app that uses AI as part of its functionality. For example, apps such as LivePlan, Bizplan, Enloop and PlanGuru use AI to generate suggested text, tidy up expression and assemble financial forecasts. In doing so, these apps can greatly streamline the process of creating a business plan.

You may wonder why I'm recommending you subscribe to a business planning app — after all, if you do so, where does this book fit into the scheme of things? What this book provides, and which planning apps do not to the same extent, is a clear sense of priorities, a strong theoretical foundation, and an emphasis on the things many business owners struggle with.

What a business planning app provides that this book doesn't are design tools to make your plan look good, assistance with polishing your English, and templates to make preparing financial projections easy.

Here are some tips for getting the most value out of any one of the many business plan apps available:

>> Try to get clarity around your business idea or business model before completing the different steps of the templates provided. An app isn't going to help you much unless you've done the hard thinking and analysis in advance.

>> Endeavor to apply the colors or fonts from your brand into the pre-existing templates supplied in the business planning app. If high-end design is key to your brand and you're pitching to an investor, you may be wise to use the app to get your plan to a certain point only, and then employ a graphic designer to create the final presentation.

>> Have a go at drafting a pitch through the app. Apps such as LivePlan include a 'pitch deck' template, helping you create a concise 'sell' for your business idea. Even if you're not looking for a lender or potential investor, writing a pitch can be great practice for framing your thinking and preparing marketing materials.

>> I sometimes like to use the app to generate financial forecasts and, once the first draft is complete, export these to Excel. From here, I can customize the forecasts further, taking time to understand the assumptions behind any calculations. (Apps can make financial reports so easy to generate that you risk not understanding the reasoning that lies behind them.)

>> AI is part and parcel of most planning apps, but you can still garner that extra edge by pasting text into ChatGPT (or an equivalent AI app) and asking for edits. For example, you might use an app such as LivePlan to help you generate your executive summary but, once you've done so, you could paste the text of this summary into ChatGPT and ask it to review what you've written.

>> Be careful that AI, along with the apps that use AI, doesn't sanitize your written expression too much, nor introduce a heap of jargon. Make sure that the clarity and immediacy of your own voice still shines through.

WARNING

Even the most brilliant business planning app won't be able to do all the legwork that's necessary, such as researching competitors, local conditions, or new market opportunities. Indeed, do be careful if using any of the industry-specific data or template text supplied, because a lot of this information is country-specific and may not apply to you.

Chapter **13**

Ten Suggestions for a Plan that's Not Shaping Up

N ew business ideas are as much about experimentation, risk and human folly as they are about prosperity and profit.

In what is hopefully a fitting end to this book, this chapter considers what to do if you aren't trading profitably, or your business plan has only served to highlight problems with your business model. When should you persevere with your business, and when ought you pull the pin? What might you retrieve from the ashes of your ideas?

Ensure You're Still Legal

What should you do if, regardless of your planning efforts, your business is trading at a loss and you can't pay your bills on time? Regardless of your personal assets and business structure, you may be subject to civil or criminal penalties if you deliberately mislead creditors. Misleading creditors includes the act of continuing to trade despite knowing that you may be unable to pay any debts incurred.

If you have a company structure, you may be wondering whether I'm correct about these possible penalties. In theory, a company structure theoretically acts to limit liability, and thereby protects the personal assets of directors. So, for example, if your company goes into liquidation, you don't stand to lose personal assets such as your home or personal savings.

WARNING

The protection offered by a company structure depends on many factors, including whether you have previously provided personal guarantees to banks, suppliers, or landlords. In addition, and of significance, this protection does not stand should you continue trading while knowing that your company is insolvent. Defining the term 'insolvent' can be tricky, but a simple definition of being insolvent is not being able to pay your debts as they fall due.

I raise the topic of solvency because this exposure of your personal assets, along with potential civil and criminal liability, is of immediate concern if your business is struggling to pay its bills on time. If finances are tight and you're continuing to purchase goods on credit, I suggest you seek professional advice in order to help assess your solvency. A tool that may be useful here is a Cashflow Projection report (a subject I explain in Chapter 11).

It may be that you can take advantage of safe harbor provisions, which are legal structures enabling you to continue trading while working on a recovery plan, or it may be that you need to take immediate steps to cease trading.

Find Ways to Take the Pressure Off

Perhaps your business is struggling because it took a while to find its feet, and during the interim period, the business sustained financial losses that continue to place pressure on cashflow. If you're confident you now have your business model working and you reckon all you need is a bit of a breathing space, your first priority is to create a Cashflow Projection report, so you can quantify your potential financial shortfall, and ascertain how long it might take to trade out of this situation.

Cashflow Projections are quite tricky to do using accounting software or a spreadsheet, so I do recommend you either get assistance from your accountant or subscribe to a business planning app. The aim of the game with Cashflow Projections is to forecast the balance of your bank account(s), as opposed to forecasting profitability.

With this Cashflow Projection as your reference point, consider the following:

>> Can you generate working capital by collecting overdue debts and tightening up credit collection policies?

>> Can you sell off old stock, even if you do so at cost or a small loss, to free up working capital?

>> How might you reduce fixed expenses, such as insurances, rental expenses, monthly subscriptions, or professional services? (If you think such expenses are as lean as can be, seek a second opinion to verify your own.)

>> Do you own any assets, such as buildings, tools, or vehicles, which you could sell at reasonable value? Would it make sense to liquidate these assets and, if necessary, lease them instead?

>> Do you have any debts? Could you look at rolling all your loans and credit cards into a single loan and refinancing at a lower interest rate?

REMEMBER

If you can't find a way to ease your cashflow situation, you do need to check that you are not guilty of trading while insolvent. Refer to the previous section in this chapter for more details.

Experiment with Margins

Does the problem with your business relate to profitability, rather than customer demand? Are you spending all hours of the day and night working, but not receiving enough return on your time to make your business worth it?

In this situation, return to Chapters 8 to 11 and experiment with pricing models and strategies. Review your pricing against that of competitors, and see whether you can sustain higher pricing, adjust pricing to charge premium services to certain customers, or experiment with sales volumes to see what impact an increase in sales might have.

Next, turn your mind to cost of sales and expenses. Can you buy products any more cheaply? How could you trim your expenses? If you manufacture items for resale, can you make the process more efficient?

REMEMBER

You can use AI apps such as ChatGPT to do some of these pricing and budgeting calculations for you. Simply send your financial reports into a spreadsheet, and then copy these results into the app, stripped of any personal details. Next, ask 'what if?' questions. For example, ask 'how much would my net profit be if sales increased by 5 percent but expenses stayed the same?' or 'how could I reduce expenses by 10 percent?'

Return to Competitor Analysis

When creating your business plan, you hopefully did some kind of competitor analysis early on, looking at who your competitors were, and trying to assess who was doing well, and why. (I talk about competitor analysis in detail in Chapter 3.)

If your business isn't working out as you planned, it may be time to step outside of the day-to-day operations and return to the research phase. Cast your net widely to look for businesses similar to your own but which, to the outside eye at least, are doing well. These businesses may not be direct competitors — perhaps they're operating in different states or even countries — but chances are they will be experiencing many of the same opportunities and challenges as you.

You may even be able to find benchmarks for your industry (a topic I talk about in Chapter 10) so that you can compare your own financial performance against that of others in a more analytical fashion.

Involve Your Team

If your business plan isn't looking too promising — whether this plan is about a proposed expansion, a new idea, or continuing to do what you already do — and you have employees, I suggest you take the time to ask for input.

Of course, you want to be selective about how you ask for this input, because you don't want to disclose confidential information or scare off employees with precarious financial scenarios. However, employees often offer amazing insights for how you might save money, reach new customers, find more efficient ways of processing orders, and much more besides. The other benefit is that by involving employees in your planning, you'll end up with a more engaged team who feel invested in helping you to make the business work.

Your team isn't just employees, of course, but may also include family, colleagues, or your accountant.

Actively Seek Expert Advice

I've observed that running a business is one of those things where people overestimate their own ability and knowledge. The adage that 'you don't know what you don't know' is so true, and many of us assume that with a combination of hard work, common sense, online resources and capital, we can do well in business and figure out things as we go along.

While you may be lucky enough for this attitude to work, if your business plan isn't on track, you're best to go on the hunt for expert advice. You may be surprised by how much you can learn, how willing people are to offer their insights, and the difference these insights can make.

TIP

Advisory centers or a business-savvy accountant are a good start for advising whether the structure of your plan makes sense, the financials hang together, and if your pricing models look sustainable. However, for a deeper level of expertise, see who you can talk to within your industry. Look for consultants who specialize in your sector, or find somebody who had a successful business similar to your own but has since retired. Perhaps look for somebody working in the same field but who is operating outside of your region and is, therefore, willing to share advice. Or, if a member organization exists for your industry, consider signing up and participating in networking groups, conferences, and other member services.

Find a Business Partner

If your plan demonstrates that your business model is strong but your capacity or resources are limited, consider seeking a partner who can buy into your business. Not only does a business partner potentially contribute capital, but in the ideal world may also have a skill set that complements your own.

This partnership approach makes particular sense if your business idea is time sensitive and you need additional resources in order to capitalize on a particular opportunity.

Know When to Call it a Day

Back in Chapter 1, I talk about something called the *anchor bias*, which is the human weakness that causes us to cling too much to the initial information we receive during a decision-making process. This bias sometimes means that business owners are reluctant to let go of their initial concept, despite evidence to the contrary, because of information they received early on that corroborated their idea.

The risk here, of course, is that people continue to throw good money after bad, stranded in a business that imposes significant costs in terms of time, money, health, and relationships.

What are the warning signs that your business model isn't working? Ask yourself the following:

>> **Is your business experiencing consistent losses over a sustained period of time?** Of course, not every business with consistent losses is a dud (think, for example, of how Amazon made a loss for the first nine years of trading). However, consistent losses combined with no significant

increase in revenue over a sustained period is clearly a red flag,

>> **Is your industry experiencing declining demand?** I talk about industry analysis in Chapter 5. If your industry is experiencing widespread decline, a swift exit is likely your best strategy.

>> **Can you pay your debts as they fall due?** If you can't, return to 'Ensure You're Still Legal', earlier in this chapter, to read more.

>> **Are you over the whole deal?** No matter the financial results, your business isn't doing what it should if you're miserable.

>> **Have attempts to adjust your business model made little difference?** If you've pivoted so often that you're almost a ballerina, but profits remain elusive, the essential premise of your business may be a dud.

I've stayed too long in two of the businesses that I've owned, and regret the opportunities wasted in each instance. I realize now that change, even when hard, brings its own energy and opportunities, and that by staying too long in a particular situation, I missed out on what this change had to offer.

Try to Sell Your Idea

Sometimes, you may not be in a position to leverage your business idea, regardless of its potential. For example, maybe you've designed a new product, but lack the capital to develop this product from its prototype. Or perhaps you have a cracking idea for a new service, but don't have access to the customer base to roll out this service on a suitable scale.

If you have some kind of strategic advantage that another company can leverage to greater success, and you can protect or trademark this advantage in some way, you may be able to sell your business for way more than if it were valued by traditional methods. I remember a colleague who started a boutique travel agency, developing a niche market for sports tours by registering a series of clever domain names. Despite four years of never making a cent's profit, this agency sold their business for a substantial sum to one of their large competitors, which was able to instantly leverage this intellectual property to generate the kind of profits the boutique agency never could.

Take the Lessons with You

If your business plan has helped you to do what's right for you, no matter whether this be a mega-expansion or the decision not to continue, then the plan has done what it was designed to do.

If you decide not to continue with your business venture, be gentle on yourself and remember that there is no such thing as failure — just as any invention usually requires many prototypes before it succeeds, so do business ideas.

Ask yourself, what's next? After all, now you understand what business planning is all about, maybe it's time to start thinking about the next idea . . .

Index

Q

quality ordered, pricing based on, 93
quantity-break pricing, 93

R

rates, using to provide consistent
  experience for customers, 48
rating your capabilities, 52–54
regional targets, 99
relationships, recognizing, 121–122
Remember icon, 3
risk
  assessing using AI, 139–140
  in strategic advantage, 20
risk-management plan, 10, 147

S

sales
  about, 87
  adding to Profit & Loss
    Projection, 130–132
  building sales forecasts, 95–100
  calculating hours in working
    weeks, 96–98
  creating month-by-month
    forecasts, 100–101
  increasing by hiring staff, 98
  predicting for established
    businesses, 99–100
  predicting for new businesses, 98–99
sales projections, 152
sales targets
  in marketing plan, 62
  setting, 67
scalability, selling, 153
securing
  business intelligence, 123–127
  funds, 81–86

SeedInvest, 84
selecting
  competitive strategies, 32–34
  pricing strategies, 88–90
selling
  scalability, 153
  your idea, 165–166
separate business, 39–40
separating
  start-up expenses, 79–80
  start-up expenses and variable costs
    from ongoing expenses, 118–119
services, costing, 105–106
setting sales targets, 67
Shark Tank (TV series), 144
side hustles, 16
SMART goals, 67, 72, 151
social media, for marketing, 68
solvency, 160
'sometimes' competitors, 27–28
sources, for creating business plans, 6–7
specialist skills, in strategic advantage, 19
Specific, Measurable, Achievable,
  Realistic and Time-bound
  (SMART) goals, 72
spouses, as a source for creating
  business plans, 7
staff, increasing sales by hiring, 98
start-up budgets, creating, 76–79
start-up expenses
  about, 75
  creating start-up budgets,
    76–79
  determining, 80–81
  securing funds, 81–86
  separating from ongoing
    expenses, 118–119
  separating start-up expenses,
    79–80
  summary of, 152

About the Author

Veechi Curtis is passionate about creating businesses that contribute to our society and help their owners achieve financial independence.

Born in Scotland, Veechi attended university in Australia where she completed both her undergraduate degree and her MBA. She has been a small business consultant for more than 20 years, training and mentoring hundreds of businesses over this time. She has written for many publications and has also been a columnist for *The Sydney Morning Herald*.

Running a business in theory is very different from running a business in practice. In *Getting Started in Business Plans For Dummies*, Veechi draws from the experience of running her own businesses, as well as being a mentor for dozens of start-ups. Veechi is also the author of *Small Business For Dummies*, 6th Edition, *MYOB Software For Dummies*, 8th Edition and *Bookkeeping For Dummies*, 3rd Edition.

Veechi lives in the Blue Mountains of NSW, where she is the executive director of Varuna, the National Writers' House.

Author's Acknowledgements

Thank you to my very silly and wonderful family, who provide me with all the inspiration I could ever need.

Publisher's Acknowledgements

Some of the people who helped bring this book to market include the following:

Acquisitions, Editorial and Media Development

Project Editor: Tamilmani Varadharaj

Acquisitions Editor: Lucy Raymond

Editorial Manager: Ingrid Bond

Copy Editor: Charlotte Duff

Production

Graphics: Straive

Proofreader: Susan Hobbs

Indexer: Estalita Slivoskey

The author and publisher would like to thank the following copyright holders, organizations, and individuals for their permission to reproduce copyright material in this book:

>> **Cover image:** © Zamrznuti tonovi/Adobe Stock Photos

>> **Table 10-1:** © Maus Software, LLC. Maus Software

>> Microsoft Excel screenshots used with permission from Microsoft

Every effort has been made to trace the ownership of copyright material. Information that enables the publisher to rectify any error or omission in subsequent editions is welcome. In such cases, please contact the Legal Services section of John Wiley & Sons Australia, Ltd.